Ian McKeever

Ian McKeever
Henge Paintings

Galleri Susanne Ottesen
Heather Gaudio Fine Art

Anomie

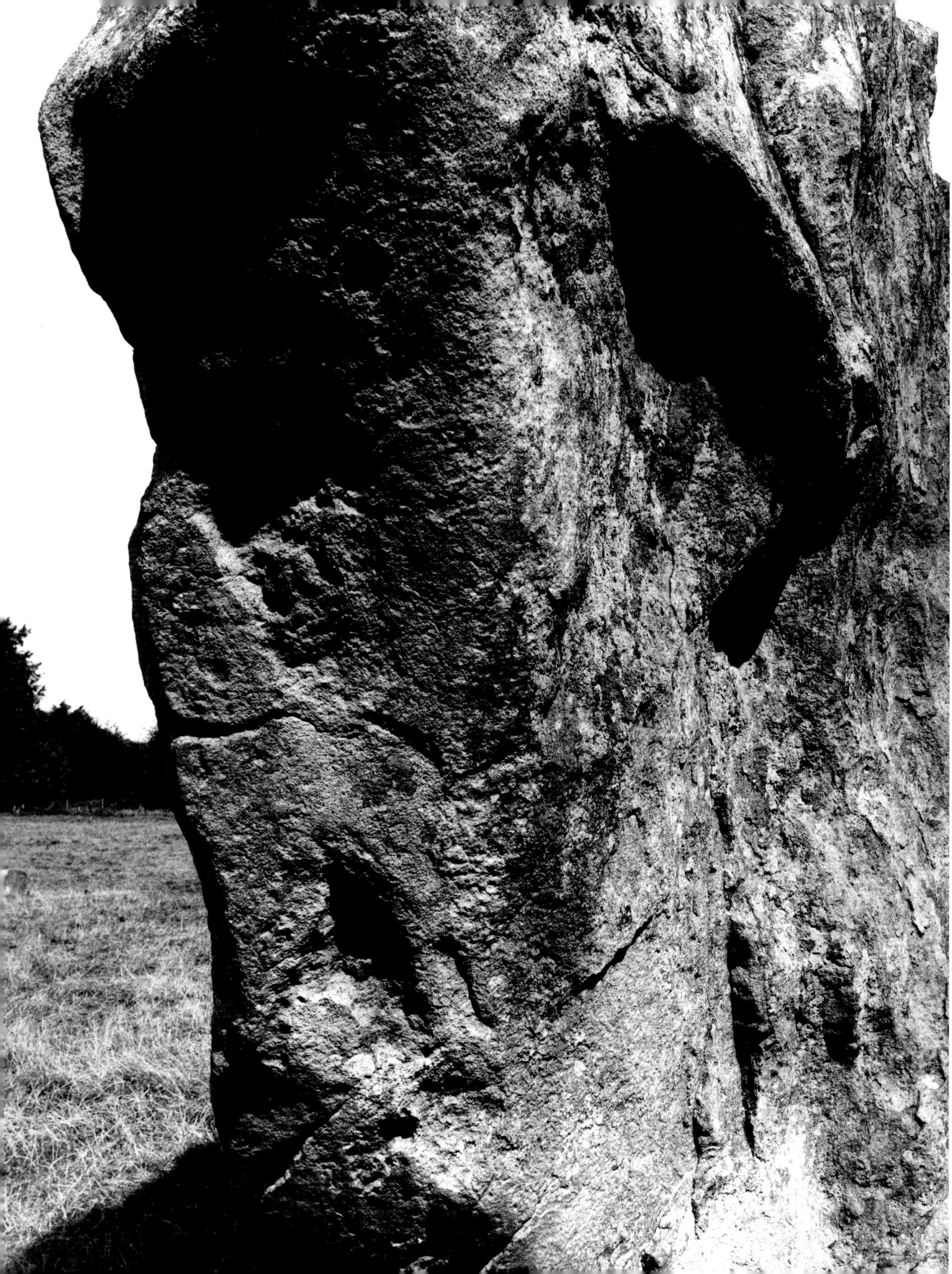

Contents

Body Forth: The Henge Paintings

Paul Moorhouse

Herbert Read described it as the moment of liberation. 'Once it is accepted', he wrote, 'that the plastic imagination has at its command, not the fixities of a perspectival point of view… but the free association of any visual elements (whether derived from nature or constructed a priori), then the way is open to an activity which has little correspondence with the plastic arts of the past.' Writing in 1959, Read defined the trajectory in modern painting which sprang from the experiments in 'pure art' conducted by Robert Delaunay, Wassily Kandinsky and others at the end of the first decade in the twentieth century. Their innovations would lead to the flowering of abstract painting, a means of expression unburdened by 'an irrelevant representational function'. Freed from imitating the observed world, henceforward artists could construct non-representational structures that would, it was assumed, 'appeal directly to human sensibility'.[1] As Read's words suggest, such ideas had a heady significance but also posed profound questions, not least concerning the capacity of abstract painting to transcend its own formal means. Can non-figurative art – a visual language of marks, shapes and colours – truly serve as a vehicle for meaning, and, if so, what exactly is being conveyed? Over a hundred years later, such questions still provoke debate. In that context, the work of Ian McKeever constitutes a compelling affirmation of abstract painting's continuing relevance in the twenty-first century.

McKeever's *Henge* paintings form the latest development in a career that spans more than five decades, and, sustaining the approach that he first adopted in 1976, the artist worked in series. Begun in 2017, and completed over a five-year period, thirty paintings were realised on three different scales ranging from the intimate to the expansive. The series is his most ambitious to date, and not only in terms of number. Surveyed as a whole, this unfolding, thematically-related body of work conveys the impression of a painter restlessly probing and interrogating issues at the heart of his own practice. Foremost among these is the matter of his work's place in the world. Having long since renounced figuration, which he regards as 'picture-making', in the *Henge* paintings he renewed his exploration of the long-standing question of how to invest his paintings with a convincing physical presence. For McKeever, this was clearly an early preoccupation. As a student, in 1967 he completed a dissertation on the work of Anthony Caro, whose sculpture addressed the very same question. For Caro, depicting figures was, as he put it, 'getting in the way'[2]: creating images of people was a form of pretence that detracted from the expressive immediacy he desired. Caro's solution was, as McKeever noted, to make abstract sculptures that possessed an independent three-dimensional reality.

For the painter, however, working in two dimensions has an entirely different character, and, as McKeever is well aware, the painter confronts challenges that are unique to the medium. The flat picture plane creates a virtual domain of apparent depth, separate from real space, into which colours and shapes recede, creating a pictorial image. The *Henge* paintings reveal McKeever grappling with this problem, seeking to imbue his work with the sense of assertive weight and personality that are attributes of real things. The question that he addressed was complex and pressing. As McKeever put it: 'How to body forth into the world?'[3] In other words, how to create paintings that possess the cogency of objects, while not relinquishing their unique character as sites for contemplation and aesthetic appreciation?

In this respect, the series is something of a departure. From 1992, not least in the *Temple* (2004–6) and *Assembly* (2006–7) series, he had made paintings incorporating transparent veils. Such works have a diaphanous quality; the shapes appear insubstantial and nebulous – ghostly apparitions floating within an indeterminate void. By contrast, the *Henge* paintings show McKeever embracing black, a colour that he associates with solidity and mass. Built up in superimposed planes, the shapes acquire an arresting sensuality, warmth, and – most surprising of all – a beguiling luminosity. Moreover, being configured as vertical forms that incline, bulge and extend, in some intangible way they possess an anthropomorphic character. Each monolithic shape has an expressive bearing, projecting an inexplicable nervous quality. The paintings transcend formal concerns, and inert structures attain a deeper, metaphorical implication, being invested with an enigmatic presence. In this way, McKeever's concern with his work's physicality has a significant undertow. By admitting references beyond the merely apparent, the paintings' allusive character may be glimpsed.

The genesis of the *Henge* paintings, as implied by their title, may be traced to a visit that the artist made to Avebury in 2016. While walking around the neolithic site, McKeever took numerous black and white photographs of the massive stones that form the three circles. He framed each megalith in close-up, their edges visible at the extremity of the resulting images. Individually, the photographs depicted, in his words, 'a body in space'.[4] Having developed the film rolls and processed the contact sheets, he then put this visual record aside. However, the experience of moving around Avebury and responding to the huge stones' monumental presence made an abiding impression that resonated with deep-seated preoccupations. 'The physicality of something standing in the world intrigues me,'[5] McKeever has commented. The large black shapes that inhabit the *Henge* paintings owe their existence, at least in part, to the mysterious, timeless objects he had observed. In common with the stones, the painted shapes are patinated – the megaliths weathered by their exposure to nature, the paintings bearing the traces of the artist's activity. Both are impressed with the passage of time, albeit on vastly different scales. The way form is shaped by external events evidently fascinates the artist and is a dominant characteristic of the *Henge* paintings.

McKeever's comment is telling in other ways, however, for it not only alludes to the mysterious physical otherness of the external world. Behind his words, there is a profound sense of personal relation to his surroundings, and an acknowledgement of the gap between the perceiver and the thing perceived. An awareness of that separation was no less keenly felt at Avebury: 'Tight up against the full body of the stones,' McKeever wrote, 'my body against the body of the stone.'[6] The difference between the two was powerfully tangible. On one side, an immaterial mind occupies a living body and apprehends something outside itself; on the other, there lies a physical reality whose essential nature remains unknowable. The dialogue between these two – a thinking, feeling observer and mute matter – also finds metaphorical expression in the *Henge* paintings.

Significantly, each work comprises a pair of elements on two panels. On one side, a black shape evokes the immutable substance of the observed world: the textured surface appears illuminated from within, its form immanent. On the other, a contrasting coloured shape – frequently white – conveys an entirely different impression. Unlike the dark solidity of their counterparts, these panels are insubstantial and weightless, suffused by light which seems momentarily solidified. *Henge VII* is an arresting example of this dichotomy: the two shapes incline towards each other but, as signalled by their separate panels, remain apart. The relation of a mind to its external surroundings, which has always intrigued philosophers, here finds eloquent symbolic expression: the two domains are almost touching – yet not. McKeever expressed this preoccupation memorably: 'I paint out of the gap between myself and the world I live in.'[7] Throughout the series, that tension and balance is maintained, forming a poignant meditation not only on the artist's experience in an ancient landscape, but on a universal human condition.

The bipartite nature of the *Henge* paintings is an essential aspect of their distinctive character, but it would be an error to regard them as diptychs. Although realised on separate panels, each painting is an indivisible whole. This apparent paradox may be understood in relation to the mind-world separation, just discussed, which is evoked by the division of each painting into two parts. The same seeming contradiction suggests a further layer of implication, which refers to the nature of each individual's being. As Descartes showed, the relation of the mind to an extended world is only part of the philosophical problem. The unfathomable connection between consciousness and the body that contains it is no less perplexing – and equally a fact of existence. This question, too, is for McKeever an abiding preoccupation. 'How to get close,' he has speculated, 'to something which is "of me"?'[8] In this respect, the duality of the *Henge* paintings is an essential aspect of their meaning, the division between contrasted parts evoking two planes of existence: the mental and the physical. Viewing each painting as one entity, we may observe – if not account for – the correspondence of thinking and feeling. According to McKeever's distinctive metaphorical iconography, immaterial light and solidified dark convey the relation of twin experiences that make us what we are: sentient physical beings.

As this suggests, McKeever's *Henge* paintings plot a course between apparent opposites. Irreducibly abstract, and comprising purely pictorial elements of colour, shape and mark, their presence – on whatever scale – is assertive and physical. At the same time, it is impossible to be unaware that the character of each work is both expressive and suggestive. Never simply formal exercises, each image has an individual personality, which is shaped by the artist's experiences, and this confronts the viewer, calling for an imaginative engagement. The paintings' potential for meaning, no less than their physical make-up, makes them what they are. In this respect, they deliver a resounding riposte to detractors who would dismiss abstract painting as without significance: among his peers, McKeever is the most metaphysical of painters. Indeed, it is clear that his aim to 'body forth' is only partly connected with investing his paintings with a physical presence. It applies equally to giving substance to thought.

What, however, is the nature of those experiences which the *Henge* paintings represent? To that question, McKeever is equivocal – and necessarily so. 'In painting a painting,' he observed, 'one does not set out to paint what one knows, but rather tries to touch those things which one does not know and which cannot be known.'[9] As this implies, he draws upon material hidden from view in deeper mental recesses that we all carry within us. When pressed, the artist avers that he never begins a painting without something, however indeterminate, on which to draw: a 'felt sensation'[10] may be the seed at the outset. Thereafter, everything that goes into the formation of an image is visible. Nothing is corrected, cancelled or taken away, and maintaining the freshness of each decision and mark is a prime consideration. In that way, the paintings are a complete record of the process that made them. In accounting for what is actually bodied forth, however, other authorities are perhaps needed, and in this respect the nineteenth-century German philosopher Arthur Schopenhauer is illuminating.

In his masterwork, *The World as Will and Representation*, Schopenhauer described the way that, beneath the surface of consciousness, there lies a mysterious mental space, which he described as follows:

> Let us compare our consciousness to a sheet of water of some depth. Then the distinctly conscious ideas are merely the surface; on the other hand, the mass of the water is the indistinct, the feelings, the after-sensations of perceptions and intuitions and what is experienced in general, mingled with the disposition of our own will that is the kernel of our inner nature… the rumination of material from outside, by which it is recast into ideas, takes place in the obscure depths of the mind.

Such material is said to be in constant motion, and, by association and analogy, there rises to the surface what the philosopher called 'the clear pictures of the imagination'.[11] McKeever's *Henge* paintings are vivid testimony to this process in action, revealing something of the unfathomable connection between the individual and the world, and the riches that lie beneath the surface of consciousness. In this respect, abstract painting begins where figuration ends, for, as Shakespeare knew, 'imagination bodies forth/The forms of things unknown'.[12] There could be no better evocation of McKeever's endeavour.

1 Herbert Read, *A Concise History of Modern Painting*, Thames and Hudson, London, 1959, reprinted 1969, pp.96–97.
2 Anthony Caro, lecture given at the symposium 'Caro, Olitski, Noland', Hartford Art School, University of Hartford, April 1994, unpublished transcript held in Anthony Caro Centre Archive, p.1.
3 Ian McKeever in an interview with Paul Moorhouse, the artist's studio, 7 March 2022.
4 Ian McKeever, email to Paul Moorhouse, 8 March 2022.
5 McKeever interview, op. cit.
6 McKeever email, op. cit.
7 McKeever interview, op. cit.
8 Ibid.
9 Ian McKeever, 'Painting is not Flat Art' in *In Praise of Painting – Three Essays*, University of Brighton, Brighton, 2005, p.61.
10 McKeever interview, op. cit.
11 Arthur Schopenhauer, *The World as Will and Representation*, vol.II, trans. EFJ Payne, Dover Publications, New York, 1966, pp.135–136.
12 William Shakespeare, *A Midsummer Night's Dream*, act 5, sc.1, l.58.

Henge Paintings

Henge I, 2017–2019

Henge II, 2017–2019

Henge XI, 2019

Henge IV, 2018–2019

Henge V, 2017

Henge XII, 2019

Henge XVI, 2020–2021

Henge VI, 2019–2021

Henge VII, 2019–2022

Henge XIV, 2020–2021

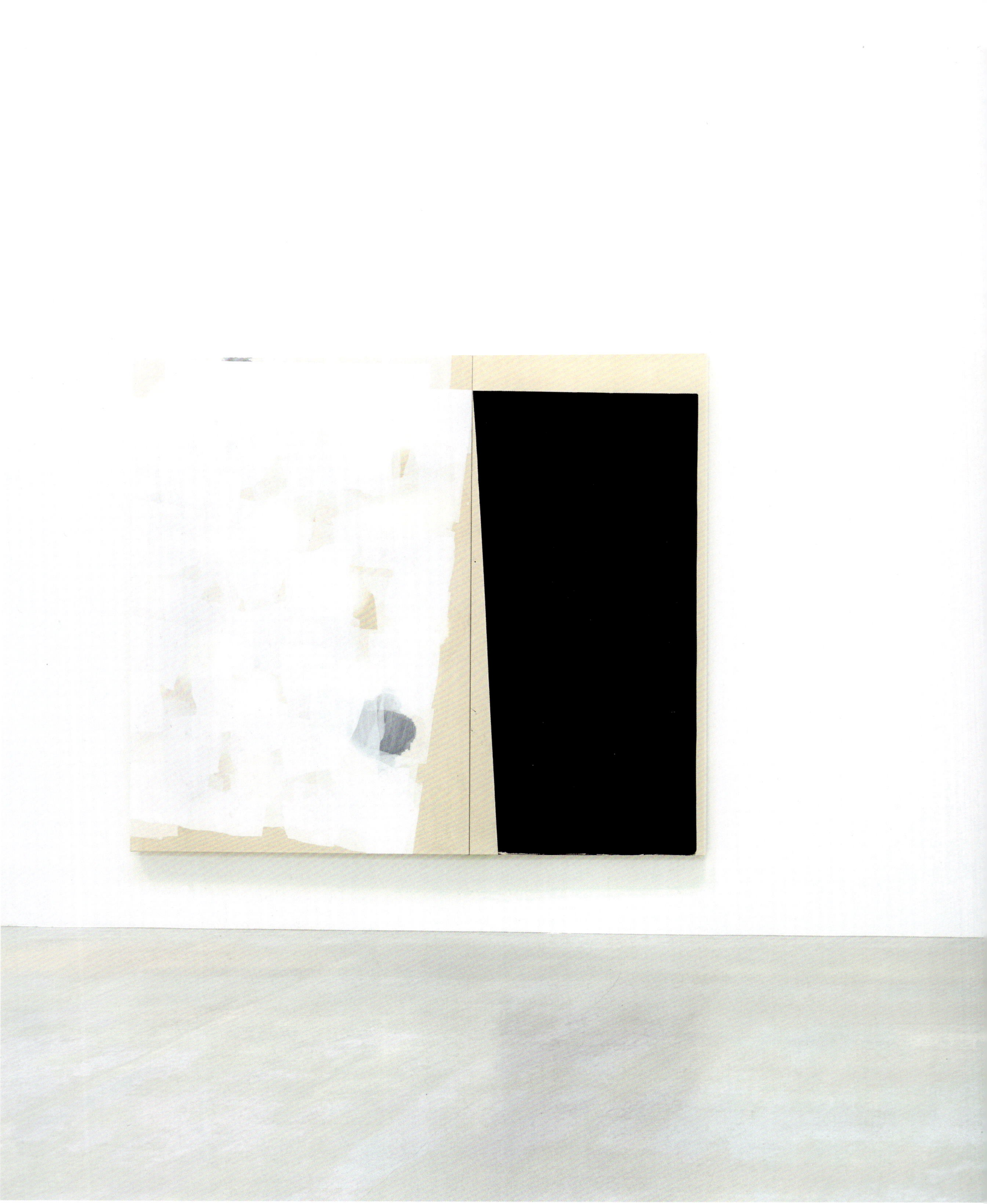

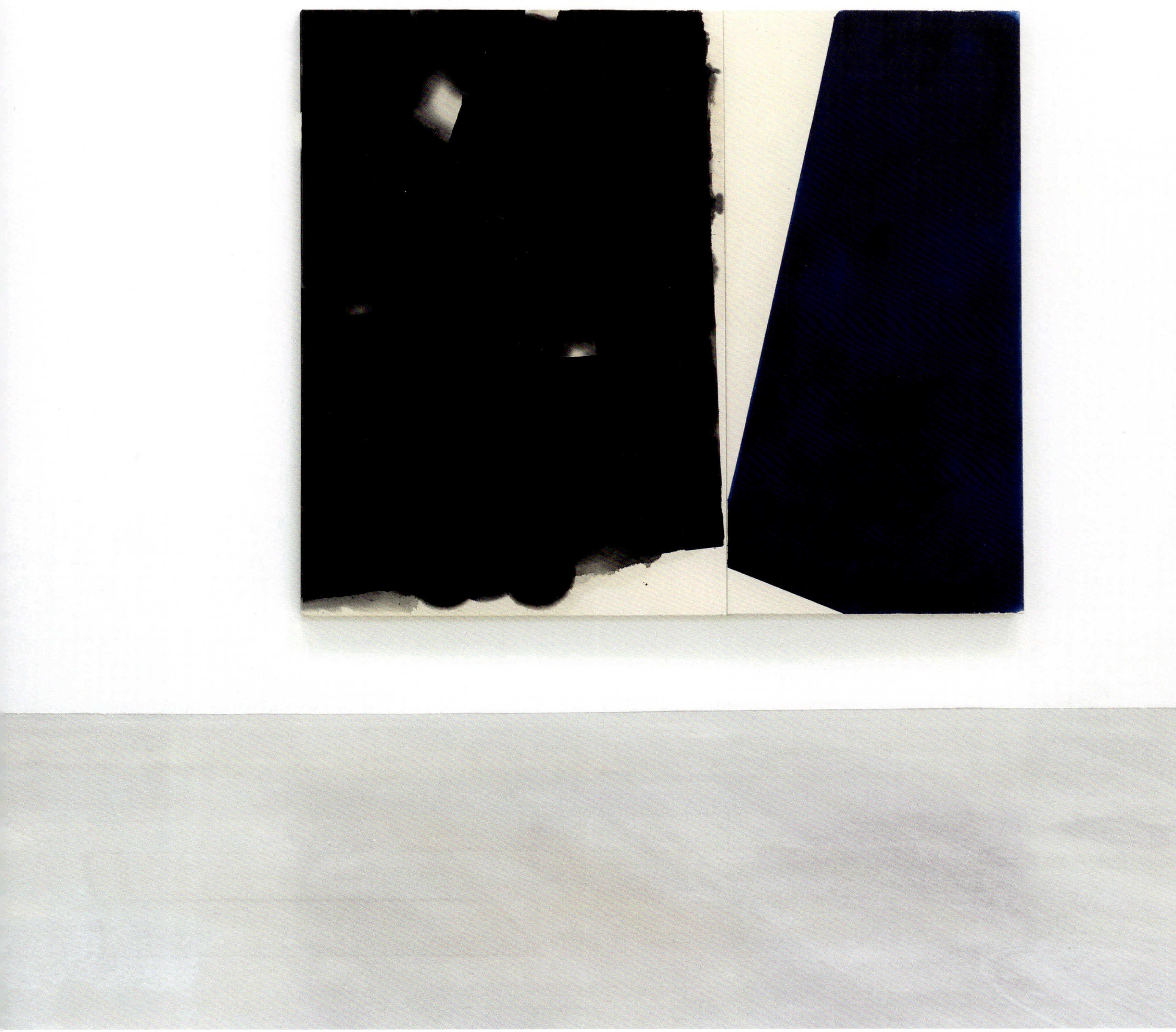

previous pages

Ian McKeever Malerei. Tony Cragg Skulpturen. Skulpturenpark Waldfrieden, Wuppertal, 2020

Henge XXVIII, 2021–2022

Henge XXXII, 2021–2022

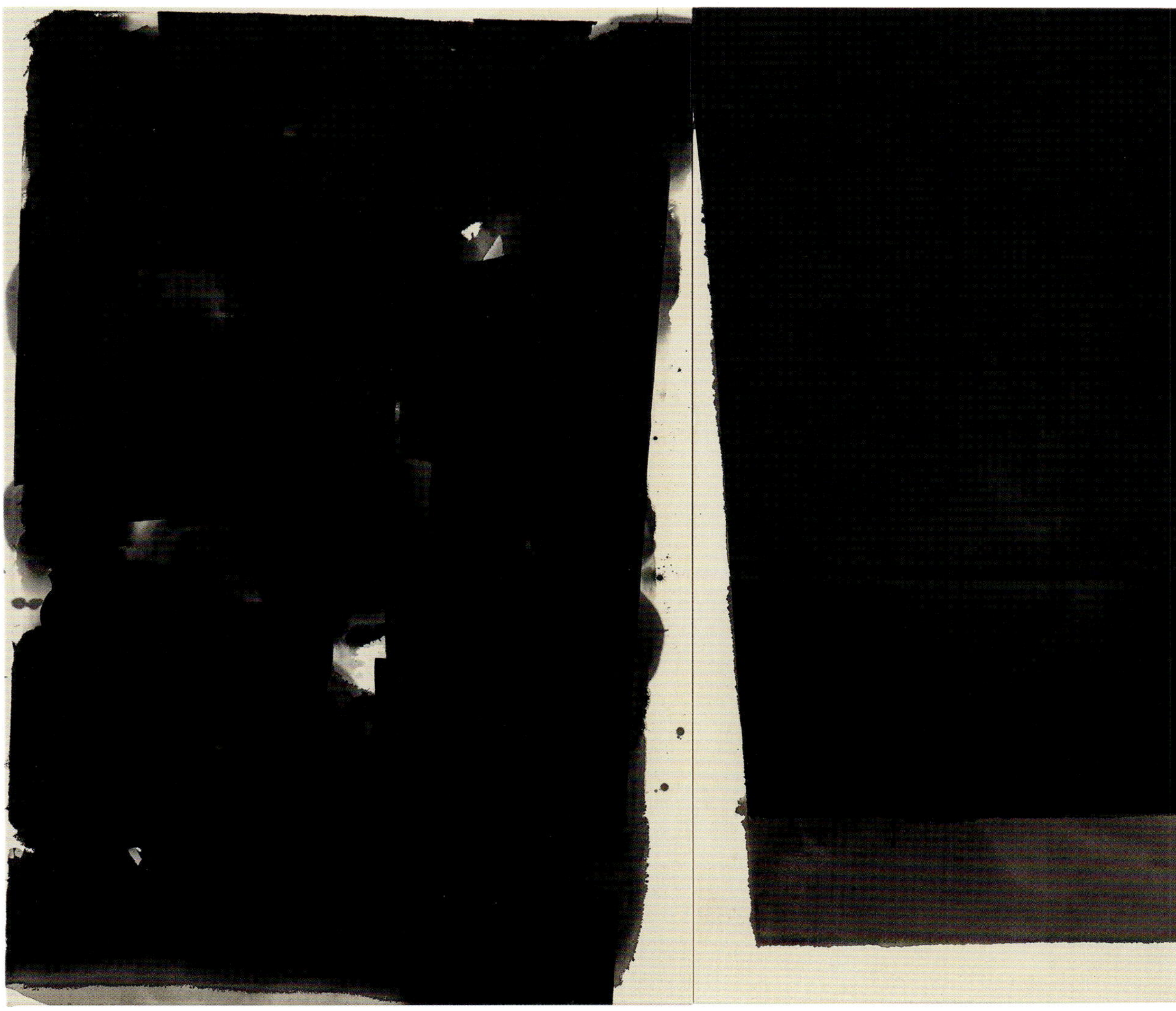

Henge XXXV, 2022

Henge XIX, 2020–2021

Henge XVIII, 2020–2021

Henge XXXIII, 2021–2022

Henge XVII, 2021–2022

Henge X, 2017

Henge XX, 2020–2021

Henge XXXIV, 2021–2022

Henge VIII, 2019

Galleri Susanne Ottesen, Copenhagen, 2020

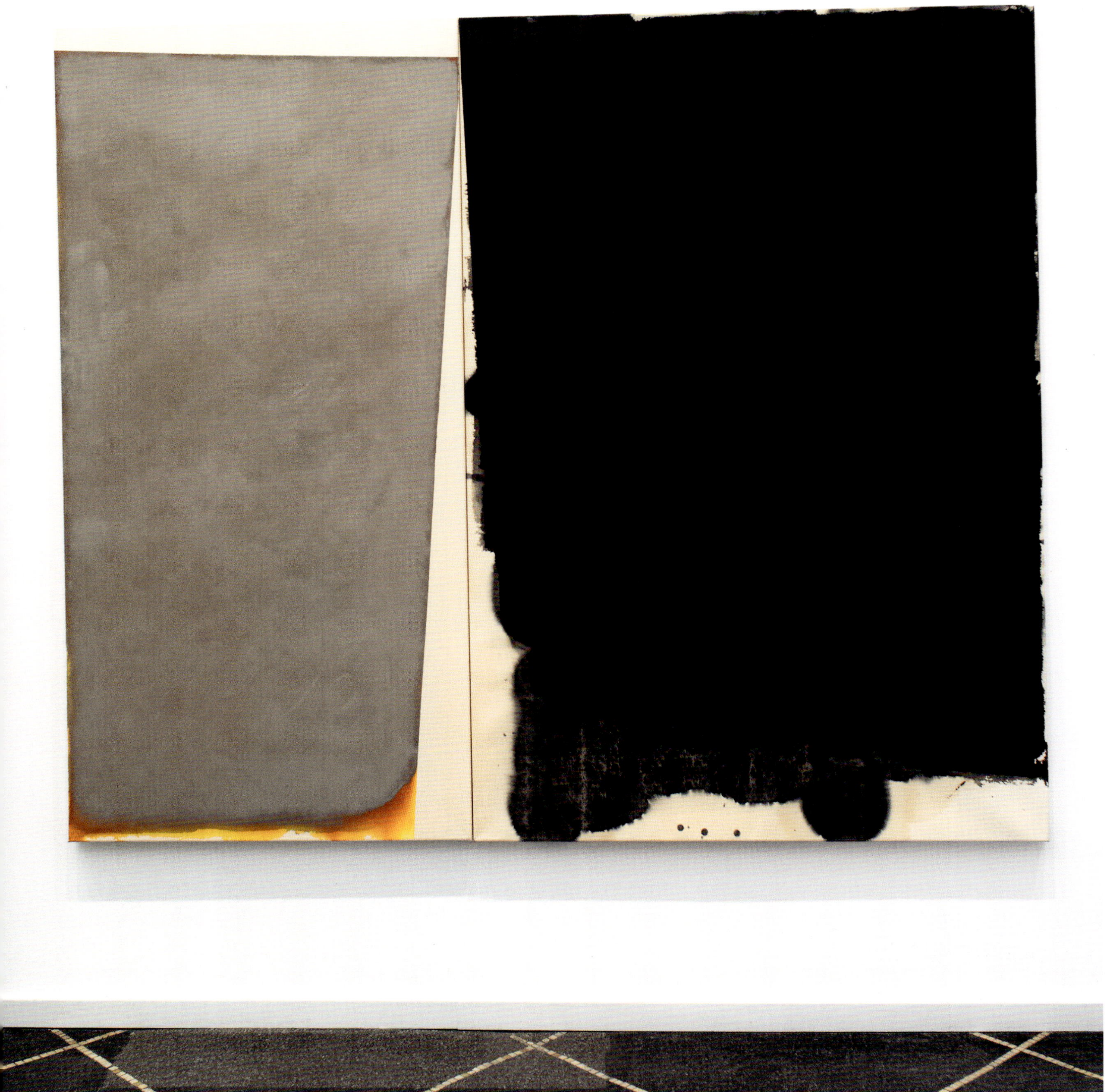

Time and Time Again

Ian McKeever

If only he could hold meaning in his hands, he thought, if only meaning were that solid, had matter. Unlike thought, which seemed so light, meaning had gravity, a sense of weight. Perhaps not easily measured, but nevertheless a weight and a form, it was graspable. He imagined taking a thought, any thought, folding it as he would a piece of paper, compressing it until it became meaning. Then holding that meaning in his hand, feeling its concreteness, its measure. Then afterwards, slowly unfolding it wide open again until meaning was no longer there, gone, and his earlier thought had reappeared. Or perhaps another thought, with which he could start the whole process of folding and unfolding all over again.

He wondered why meaning was always smaller than thought. What happened in the shrinking transfer from one to the other? Did the shift of thought to meaning open up another kind of gain? Or was that transfer with the passing of time simply the gaining of weight? He knew that time was important in this exchange, yet could not see how. Time was too big, distant, remote even, to be held in any space meaning might occupy. It was so much bigger than space. And anyway, time never settled, never committed to one place, it was always just passing through.

Time and time again, like his piece of paper, he tried to fold the thought, to give it weight. Compressed, it now had meaning yet strangely was displaced outside of time. He held it in his hand, feeling its weight, observing its form. Then slowly he began to prise open the parcel of meaning. Now open, he waited. Waited for time to become thought again.

He looked at the painting on the wall. Thought leaned into meaning. It would change things. He did not know how. He could sense it changing shape, becoming more rounded. He would not rush it; no, let it settle. There had been a time when he would have. Not let things settle down first, that is. Now he gave in to the lean. Felt its implied heft and mass. Up against it, meaning became solid, ceased being between things and became state. He could feel it as he rubbed against meaning. The rub gave it both form and solidity. The refrain from the song 'Lean on Me' came to mind. Now settled, his thoughts drifted.

Works on Paper

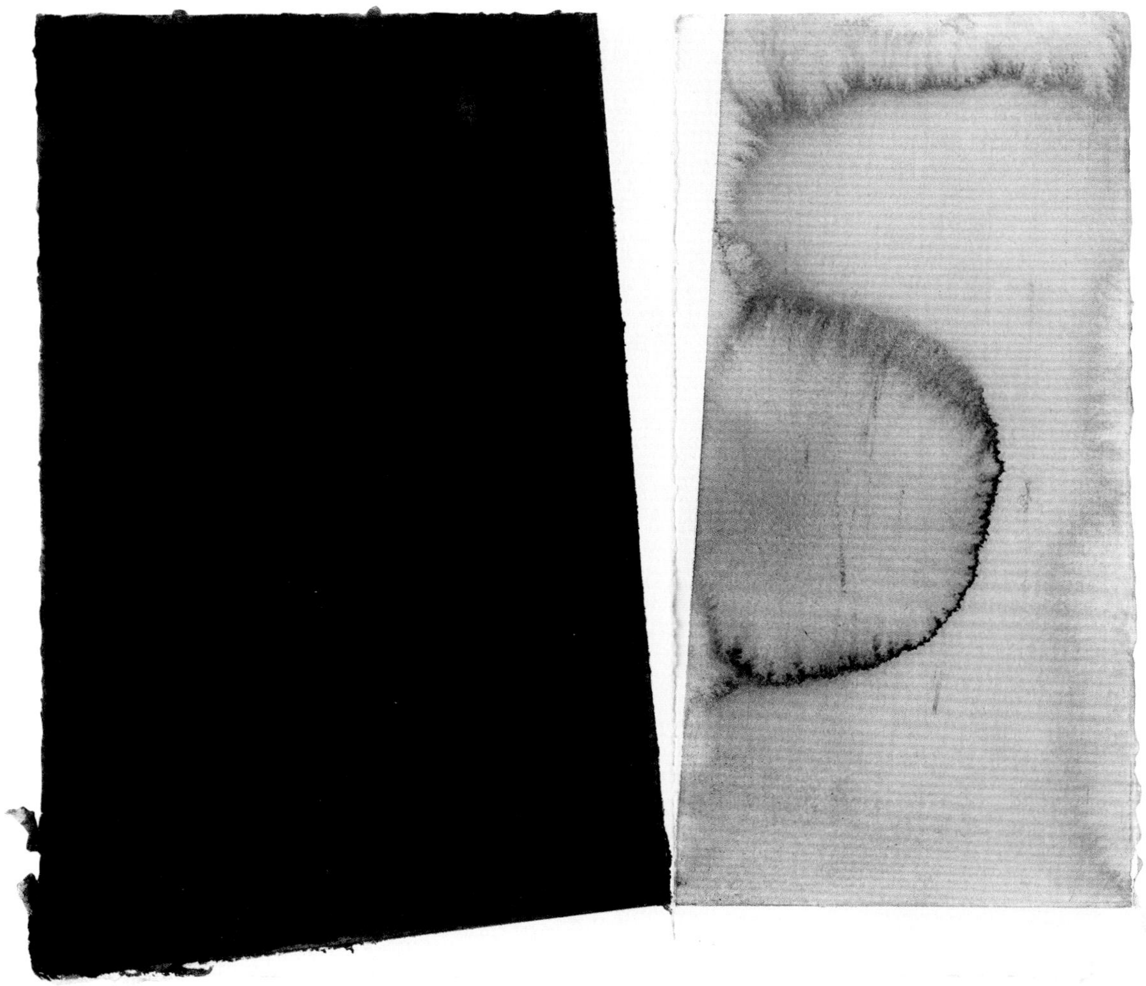

Henge No. 8, 2021

Henge No. 4, 2021

Henge No. 2, 2021

Henge No. 3, 2021

Henge No. 7, 2021

Henge No. 6, 2021

Henge No. 5, 2021

Henge No. 1, 2021

Henge No. 9, 2021

On Sculpture and Painting

Ian McKeever in conversation with Jon Wood

Jon Wood: *I would like to start this conversation about your interest in sculpture – and about the sculptural in your work – by asking you if you sometimes feel a greater affiliation with sculptors than painters?*

Ian McKeever: Yes, I think I do, certainly in more recent years. I'm drawn to sculpture for what it basically is: a fully formed three-dimensional object standing free in the world. In the contemporary context, I feel a greater affinity to the work of Tony Cragg and Richard Deacon, for instance, or, looking a little further back, to Eduardo Chillida, than I do to most contemporary painting. Good sculpture still holds presence before it has meaning, although perhaps 'fool's gold'; I would wish this for painting as well, something that I think it used to have. Painting today is more engaged in the fictive world of image-making. The painting has become foremost a picture, just another image in a world full of pictures.

JW: *It was interesting to see your* Henge *paintings on display in the company of Cragg's sculpture at Skulpturenpark Waldfrieden in 2020. I thought they worked well together. They seemed to come off the wall: very physical, solid and textured. How did you think they worked in that context?*

IM: The surface of the paintings is an emphatic two-dimensional plane, and the paint is applied in thin layers. In that sense, in the first instance texture is visual, not physical. The 'bodying forth' they suggest is held on a flat plane, as the paintings are wall-bound. This is the strange paradox in painting. The Cragg sculptures sit with unequivocal three-dimensional presence in the space, and I find their solidity very affirming. Also, they're made of wood, emanating a certain warmth, which is a quality I need to respond to work. The largest sculpture, titled *Sail* [2017], is over three metres high, roughly in the shape of a mandorla; its modulating, almost pearlescent white surface feeds right back into the paintings. Things connect and there is a real dialogue.

JW: *Whiteness was a striking quality of that exhibition, not only between the sculptures* *and the paintings but also, of course, through the interior of the gallery itself. It was something you mentioned at the time, too. How do you tend to think about whiteness and the issues it raises for painting and sculpture?*

IM: At the opening of the exhibition, I spoke about the nature of white, my experience of walking into the bathroom and listing the different whites one comes across: the colour of the walls, the tiles, towels, toothpaste, soap and so on. Not only do they all have a different quality of white, but because of the material used, they hold white in unique ways. As a colour, white is so nuanced, easily inflected by the surface containing it and by what is around it. Pure white is more a matter of the mind than actuality. I think the purest white I have ever seen is that of an orchid. In terms of painting, white expands, it is breathing out as if emitting an inner light. It's a colour I have worked with extensively for many years. I'm not sure I understand how it works in terms of sculpture; certainly it takes away weight. At the same time, white can suggest a luminous core: here I am thinking of some of Chillida's alabaster pieces. Or in the case of Cragg's *Sail*, it's like a bar of soap or a candle, the way such things seem to hold the colour internally as opposed to being simply a painted surface.

JW: *I'd like to hear your thoughts on sculpture's famous (or infamous) weight. I'm interested in how these thoughts relate to your own paintings and to those works of other artists that have struck you over the years.*

IM: I think sculptors wear boots and painters wear shoes, they somehow stand differently in the world. Regarding sculpture and weight, I'm not sure I do understand it. If I think of the work of Cragg and Deacon, then I see Cragg as emerging from the ground, the work is rooted, while Deacon's sculptures find form more from the mind, to then seek placement. My own concerns cut right across this difference, rising and falling – the placement of a body, so to speak. An important image for me when I was younger was the documentary photograph of *Asphalt Rundown* [1969] by Robert Smithson: how gravity was allowed to find its place, be both visibly and physically present. So much painting appears to deny gravity, is afloat in pictorial space. I'm uncomfortable with this; gravity's presence is crucial for me. Also, when a work gets too big, it ceases to relate to the human body and loses this physical pull.

JW: *That's interesting and makes me think of many so-called 'sculptors' drawings', in which sculptors seem to relish the free-floating, gravity-defying possibilities of the page and of being liberated from the pull of the earth. Photographs of sculpture do the opposite, further heightening our sense of sculpture as being grounded and highlighting intricate relationships with its material context. Your fascination with Smithson's work seems key here, and I wonder if photography has often mediated your appreciation of sculpture and its values and, in turn, helped coordinate the place and predicament of your painting.*

IM: If I look at the photograph of *Asphalt Rundown*, then I do view it in terms of painting. The work becomes planar. What's interesting about sculptors' early use of photography – as in, say, Auguste Rodin, Constantin Brâncuși or Medardo Rosso – is that they reduced a three-dimensional object to a plane, and something interesting happens in that gap from 3D to 2D. Even if one thinks of the photographs of Barbara Hepworth's work in the studio, one is looking differently from how one understands the work in the flesh. Painting, in being two-dimensional, doesn't have this frisson, the painting and photograph all too easily meld, blur into each other, the distance is not there. Although I haven't thought about this before in terms of how sculpture relates to photography, perhaps my own approach to it and my understanding of sculpture is informed by this difference. In my own use of photography, I've never wanted to blur the boundaries between it and painting, but to see it as something other than painting. I think there are some sculptors who think like painters, and some painters who tend to think like sculptors, and there's probably an element of this in my paintings. The sculptor is body-to-body with his or her work, their own body in relationship to that of the sculpture; painting goes from body to plane, the

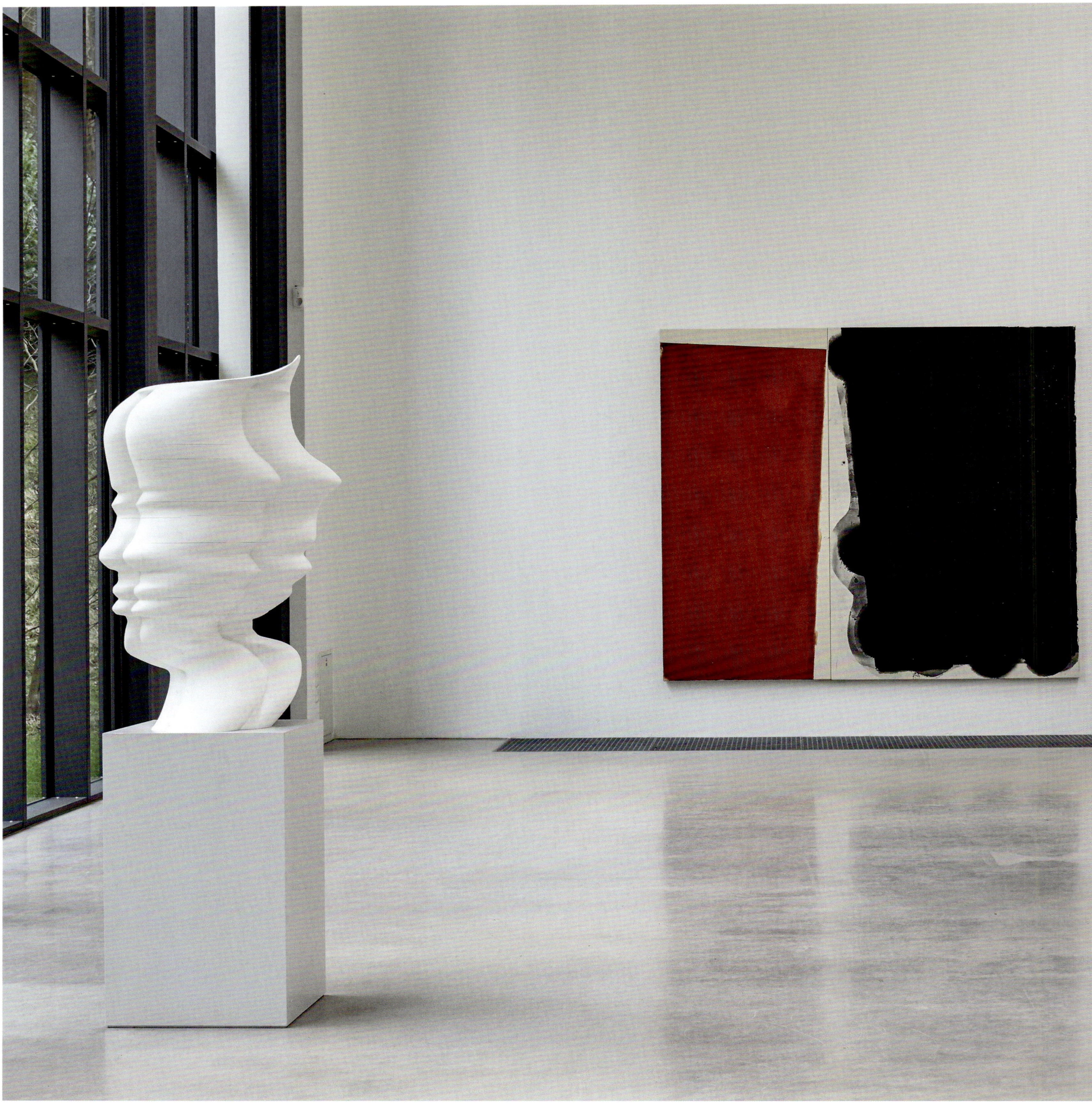

Ian McKeever Malerei. Tony Cragg Skulpturen. Skulpturenpark Waldfrieden, Wuppertal, 2020

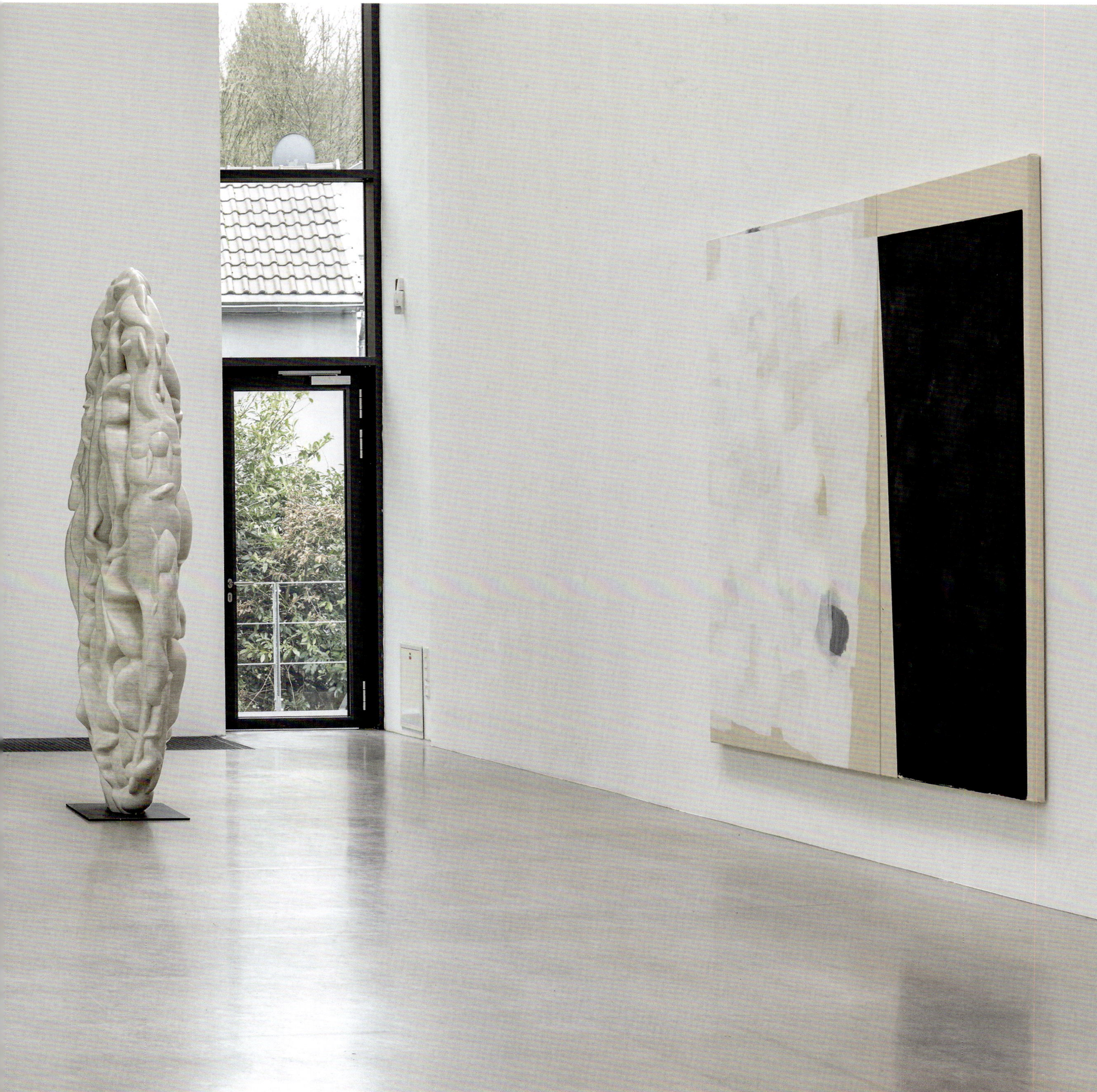

surface of the painting. I see the photograph, including sculptors' photographs, as a means of negotiating that difference.

JW: *Please say more about how photography has helped you negotiate two and three dimensions and the differences between them and paintings and sculpture.*

IM: In simple terms, photography gives distance. What is photographed is always out there, separate. Painting doesn't have this distance, it's more intimate in the sense that one cannot – at least, I cannot – separate myself from it. There is always a bodily connection, the painting rubs against one, in a way that I don't think photographs do. Also, the photographic image is held in the moment, the moment of taking. The painting's sense of time is different; time sits in painting in a different way. I think that time is more important and, actually, more evident in painting than is space. Time is what we get when we begin to look at a painting, and its significance is much underrated. I'm not sure how this relates to sculpture. Sculpture is objectified in a way that painting isn't. It has a concreteness. Perhaps here, there's a connection between sculpture and photography to do with making concrete, making real, which has to do with a certain sense of time, a time not so readily available to painting. I can't say I understand it, but it's something I sense. Often, I think the speed at which the materials used in sculpture and photography move is faster than in painting.

JW: *How do you think of the materials of sculpture as moving faster?*

IM: Certain materials just feel faster than others, for instance I think steel is faster than either stone or wood. Perhaps it has something to do with touch. To what extent the material engenders the desire to touch or to hold. The desire fosters a slowing down. It's curious that sculpture sits but encourages movement. The surface of the painting, its material flatness, induces stillness in looking. The implied body of the painting and the body of the viewer somehow hold each other. Paintings are never touched, yet I think good paintings do somehow engender a sense of touch, what

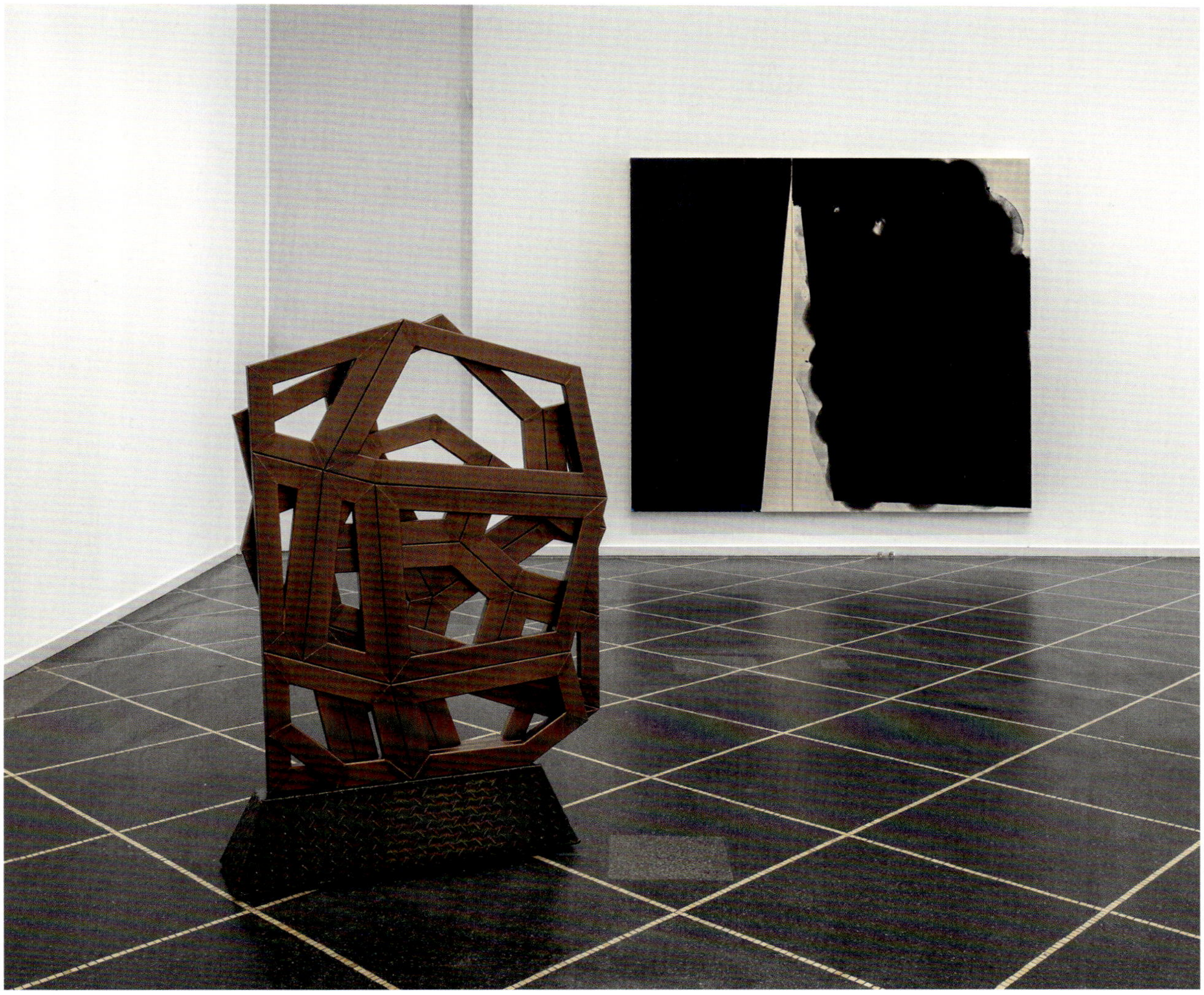

Richard Deacon & Ian McKeever, Galleri Susanne Ottesen, Copenhagen, 2018

we might call the 'feel' of the painting. I'm drawn to a painting's presence, which at its best moves from the physical to the metaphysical, if that's not too grand a term.

JW: *It's interesting to come back and think about the* Henge *paintings in relation to this 'feel' of the painting. They are black and white worlds – both the paintings and the photographs. Perhaps you could share your thoughts about this ongoing tendency in your work in relation to this 'sense of touch'.*

IM: Perhaps at its core, it's what I alluded to earlier: the paradox of the painting being essentially a two-dimensional plane, yet the painter wishes to evoke, to bring into being, a truly physical presence, as real in the world as you or me. My use of a limited colour palette, mostly black and white, is, I think, foremost physical, felt. The differing ways black and white hold weight, the light, density, suggest form, the coming into being or receding of things, so to speak. Painting for me functions at the liminal edges of things. In that sense, paintings are edgy, brittle, fragile even, what can be grasped is febrile. Black and white seem to say more about this condition, they allow me into a greater sensed proximity, to get closer edge to edge.
JW: *As we bring this conversation to a close, I want to ask you about Stonehenge. I know you live quite near Avebury and Stonehenge and have visited these sites a number of times over the years. Nena Dimitrijević once wrote that there is no Altamira or Lascaux in the British Isles, but there is however Stonehenge, Avebury and Silbury Hill, and that maybe it's this that has determined the course of modern art in this country. What do you think about this idea? She says 'modern art', although she was writing in the sculpture exhibition context.*[1] *Do you think it might apply to painting and sculpture?*
IM: That's a big question. One certainly senses a deeper connectedness to Britain's ancient past in sculpture than one does in painting. The megalithic sites, structures, even later architecture somehow still seem to be in dialogue with sculpture, whilst it is difficult to sense this same thread in painting – but then, after all, the old stone sites are sculptural in the broadest sense. One has to remember that the British painting tradition is relatively recent. It's something like room 30 in the National Gallery before one gets to British painting in the eighteenth century with Reynolds, Turner or Constable, for example, and in the meantime one has walked through the whole of the great European painting tradition. The painting tradition here, like the literary tradition, is very narrative based, abstract thought is an anathema. I, however, essentially work with abstractions in one form or another. I've lived in

rural Dorset for over thirty years, and this somehow gives a different sense of time, perhaps more so than of place. My interest in alluding to early megalithic sites in titling the group of paintings *Henge* paintings was in touching that deeper sense of time, time's weight, so to speak. How to imbue a painting with its own weight of time, forsake the immediacy of the here and now.

1 Nena Dimitrijević, 'Sculpture and its Double: Towards a Definition of Post-Evolutionary Sculpture', in *The Sculpture Show*, Arts Council of Great Britain, London, 1983, p.137.

Ten Stones

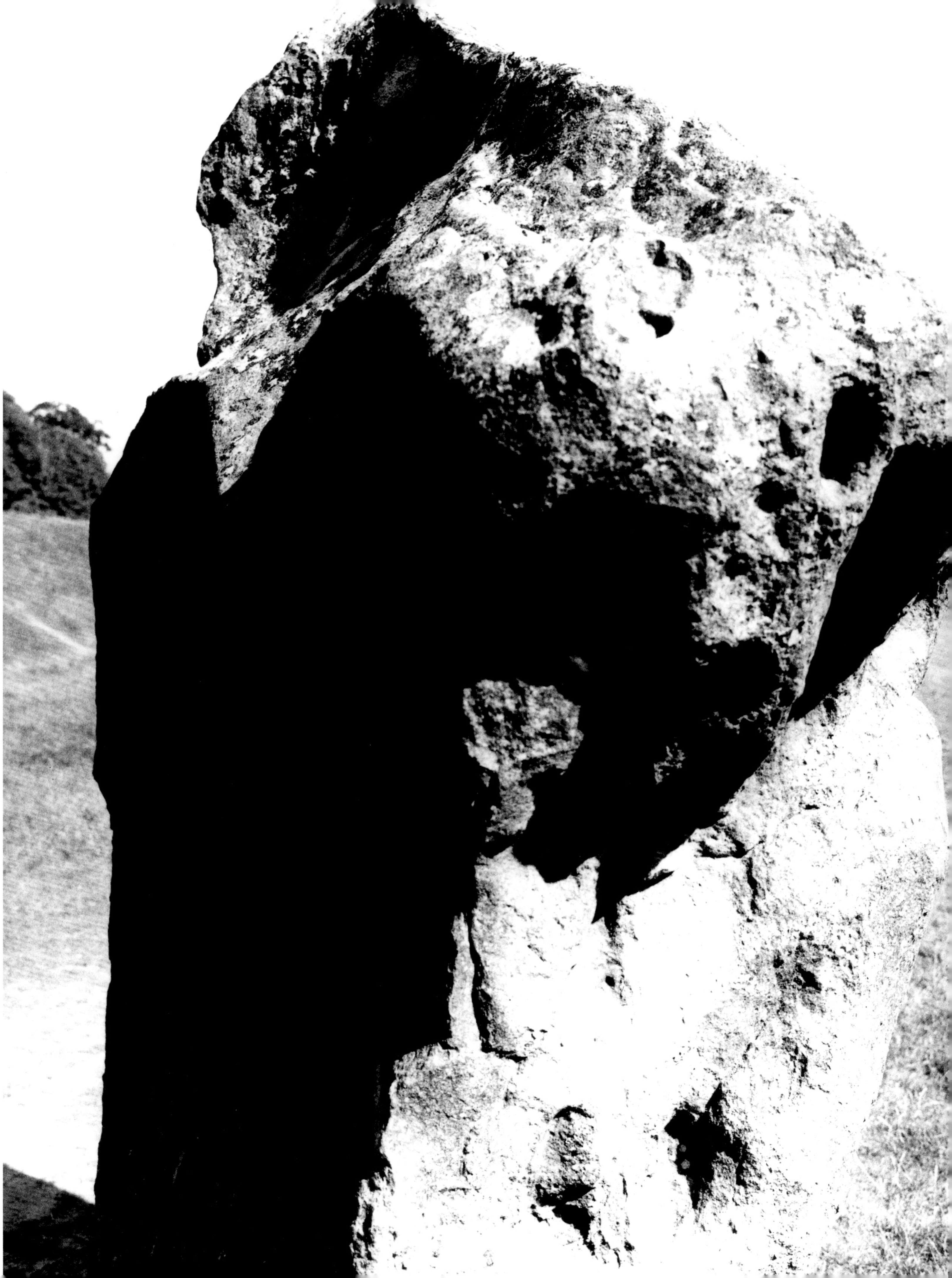

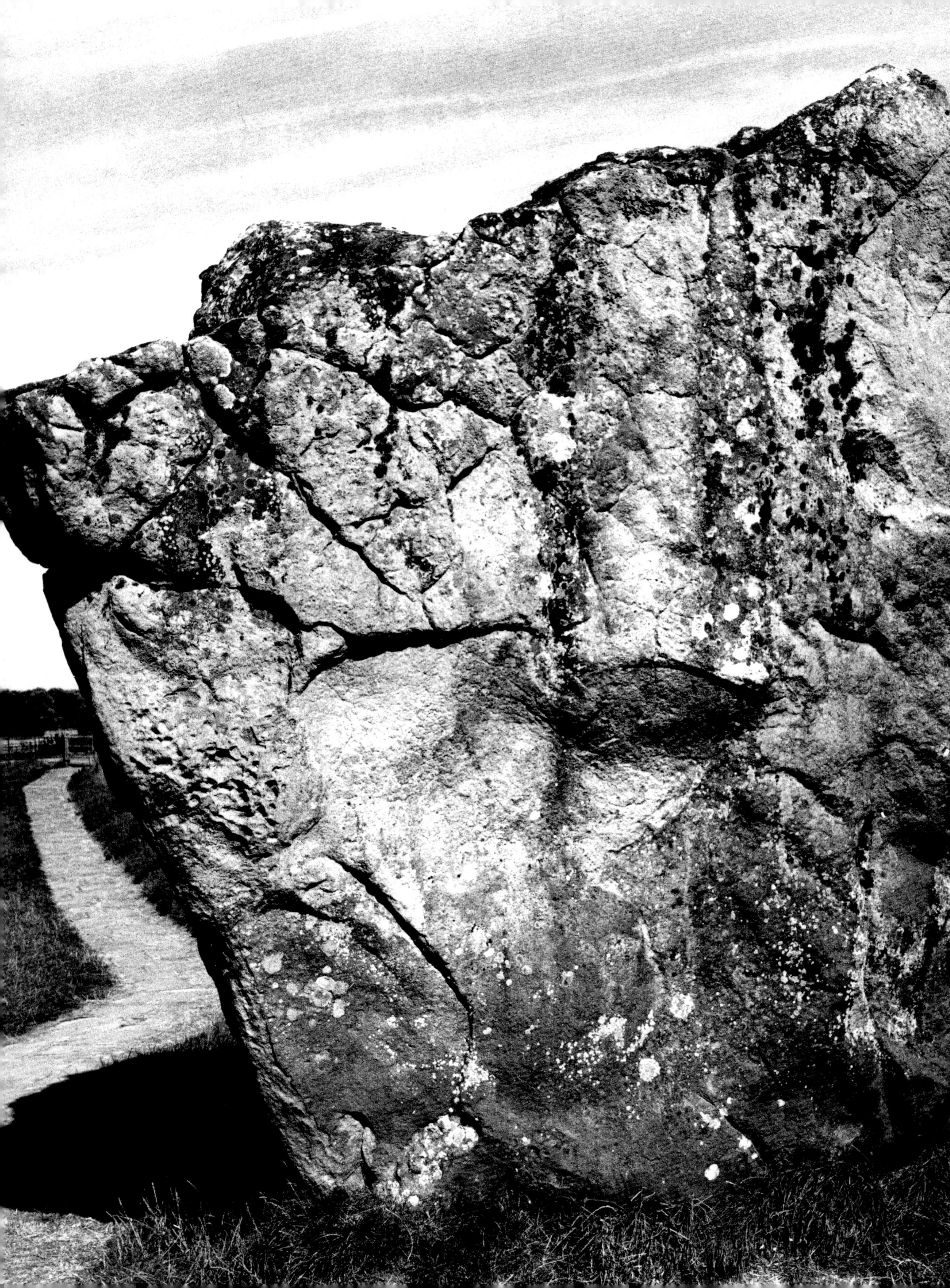

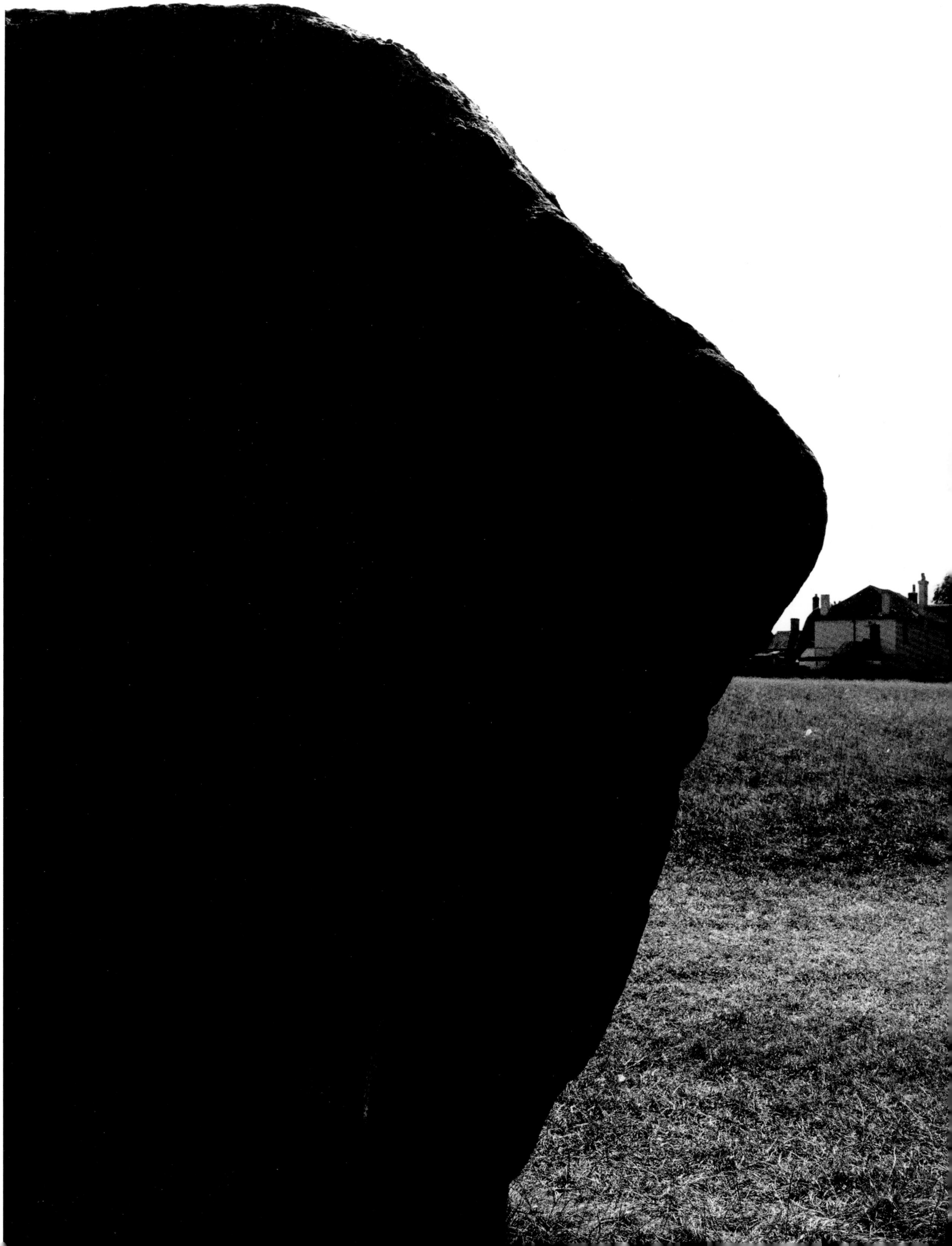

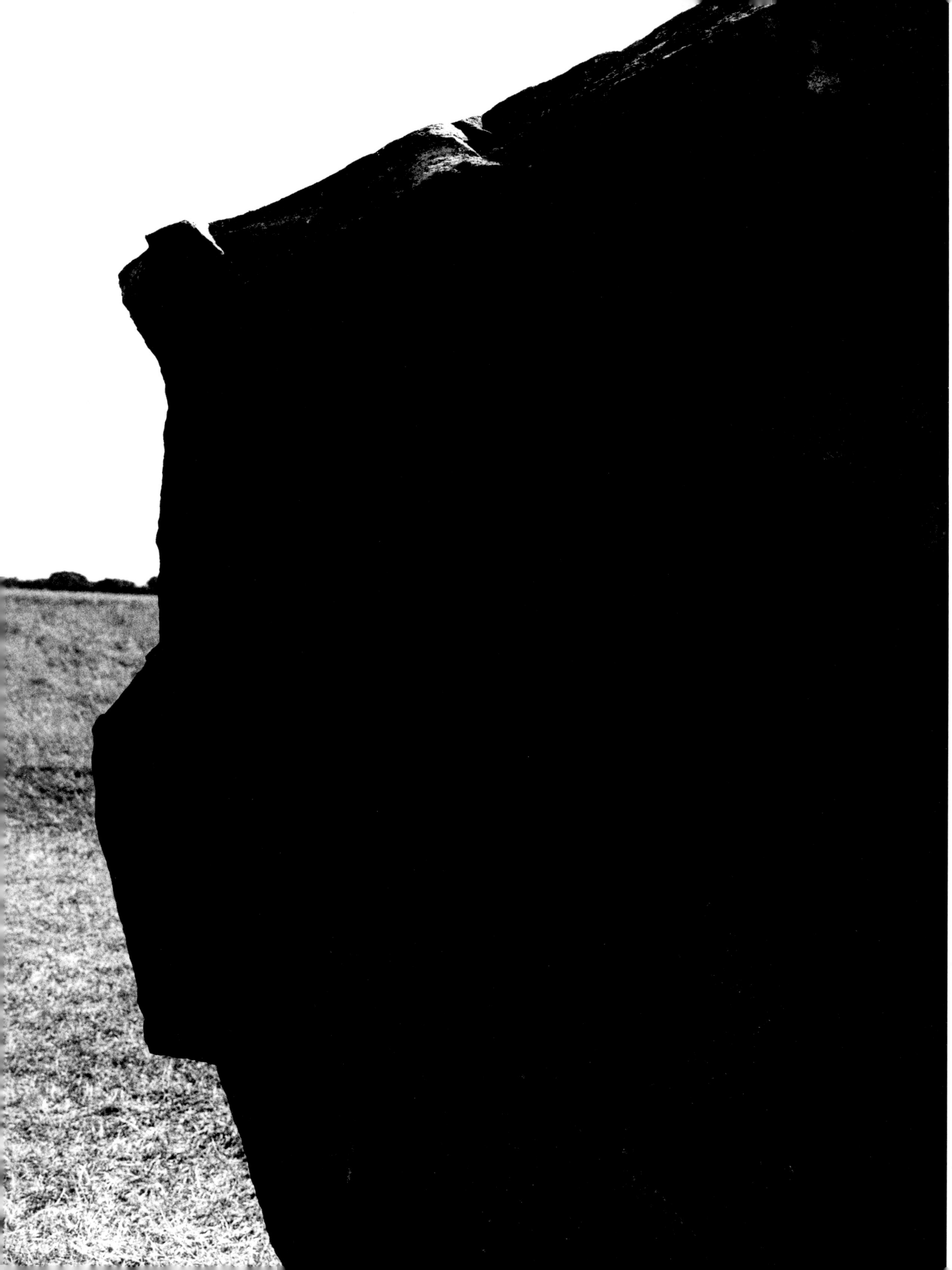

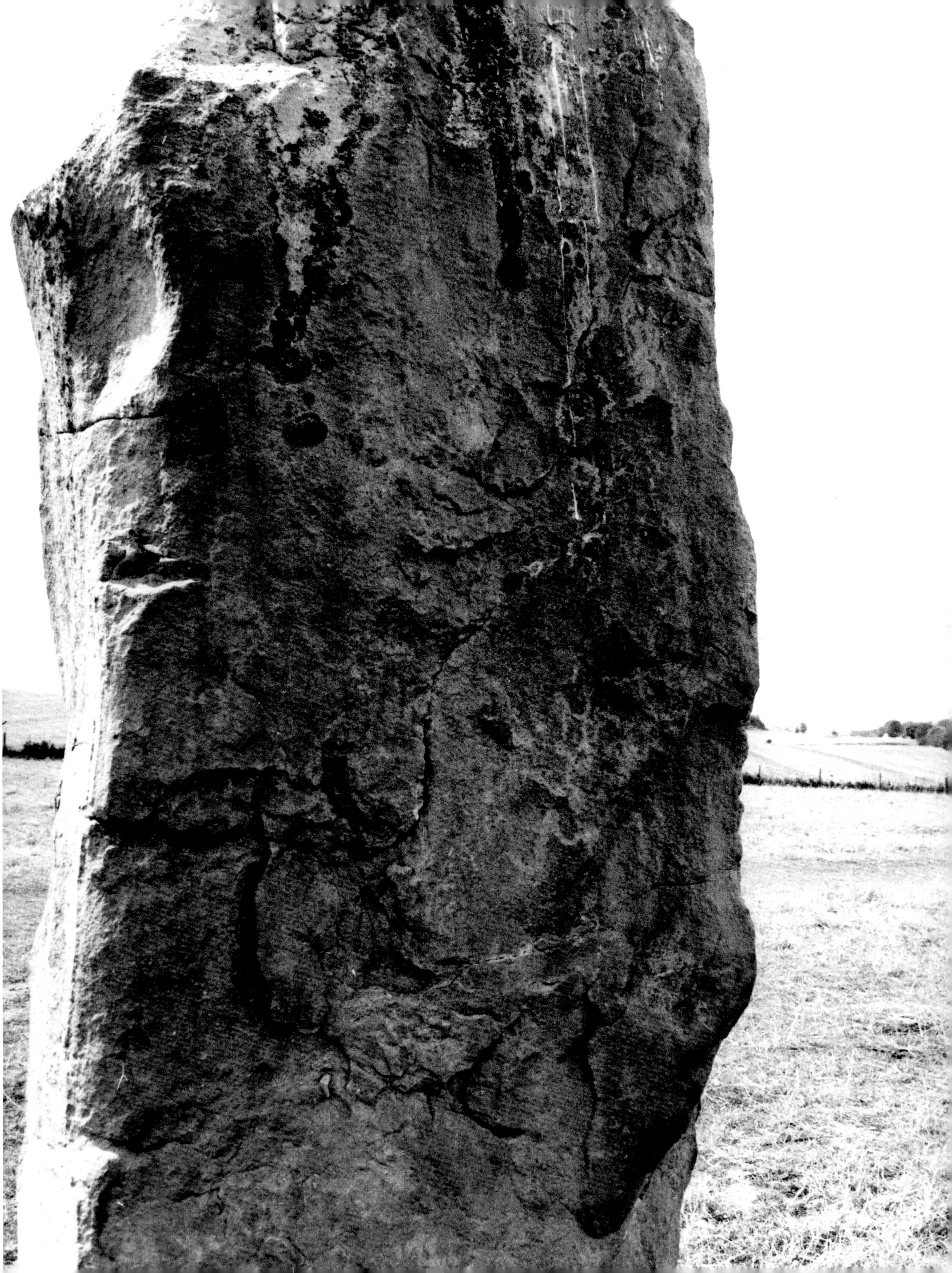

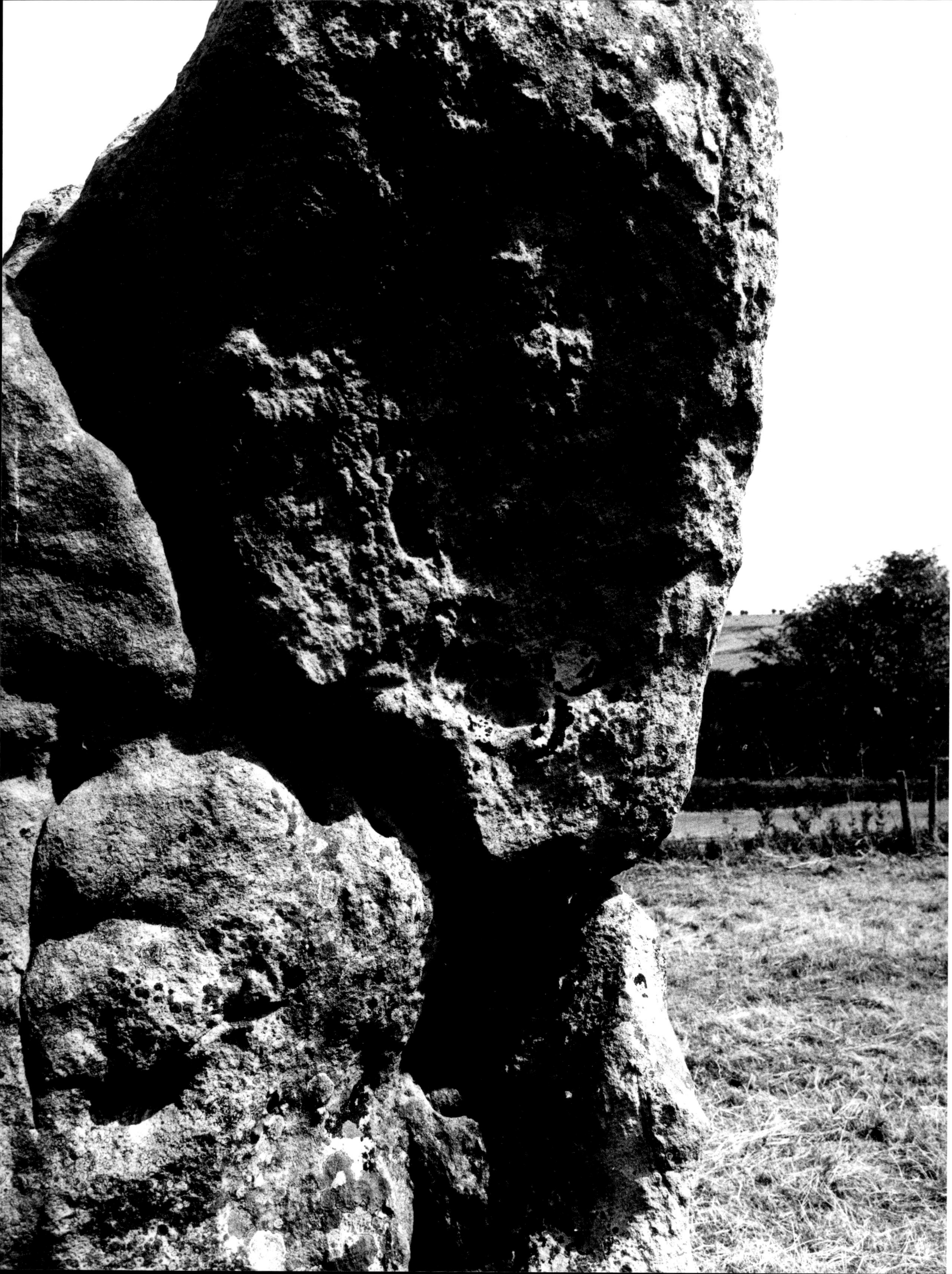

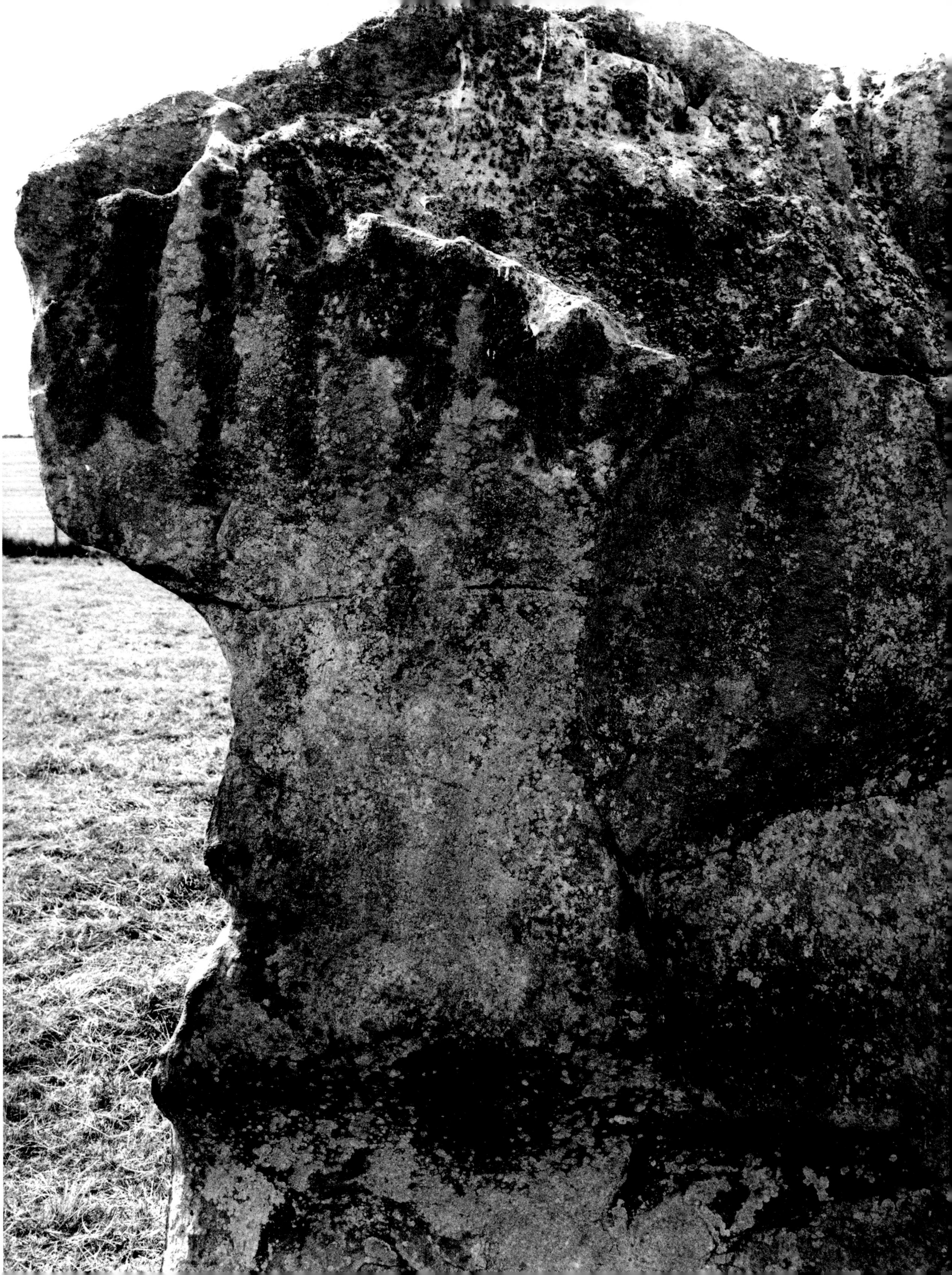

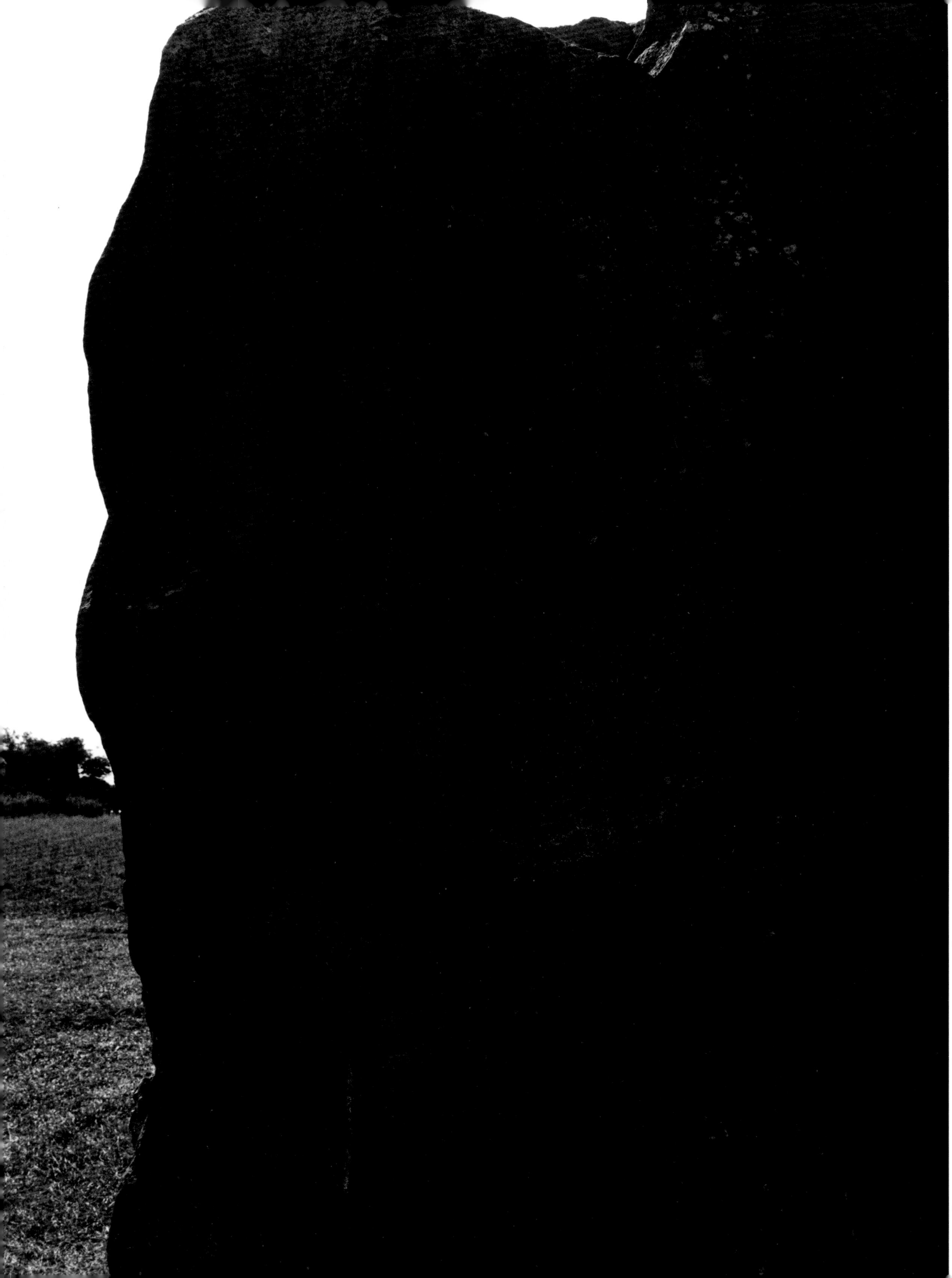

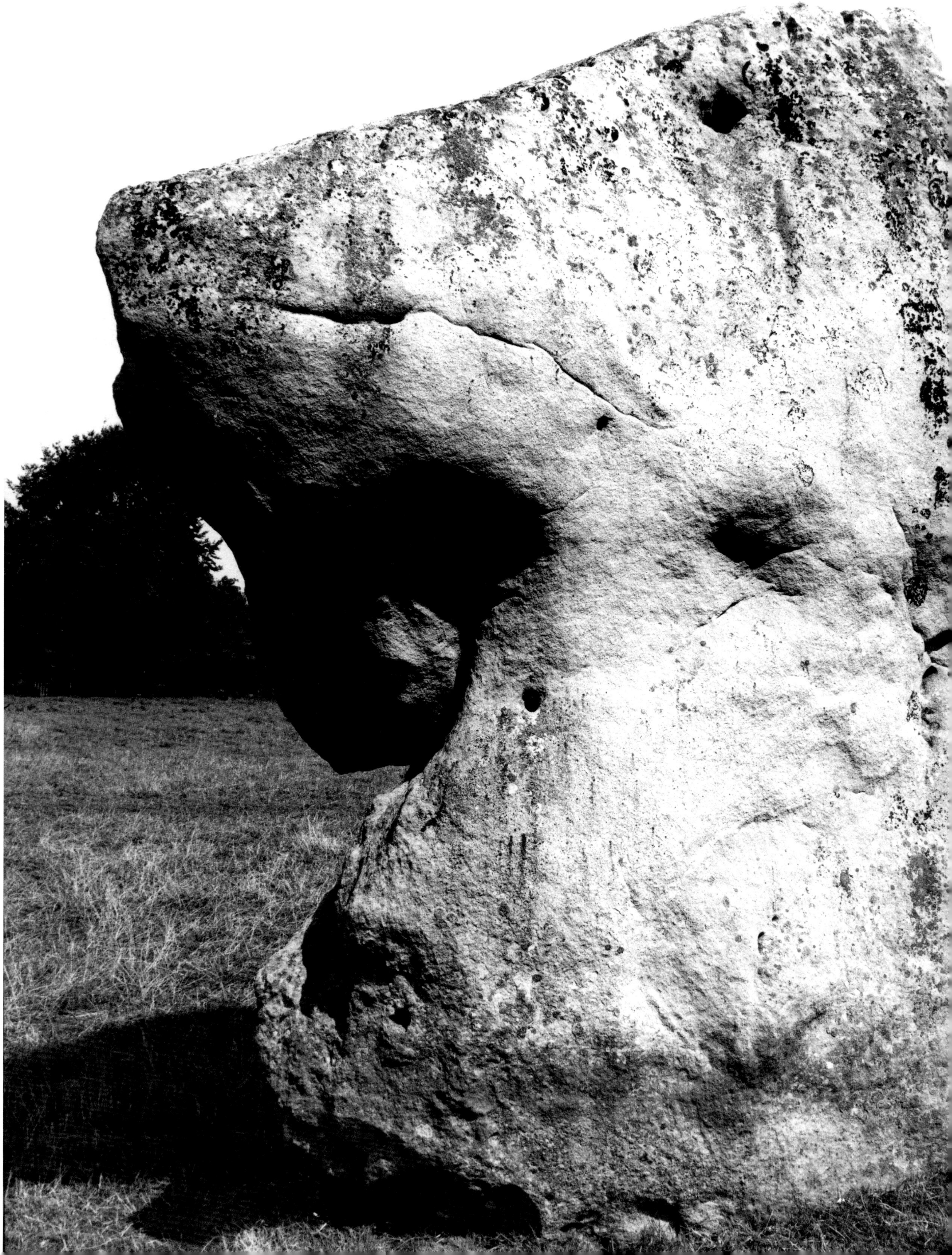

Work List

Paintings

p.17
Henge I, 2017–2019
Acrylic and oil on canvas
240 × 285 cm
(94.5 × 112.2 ins)

p.19
Henge II, 2017–2019
Acrylic and oil on canvas
240 × 285 cm
(94.5 × 112.2 ins)

p.21
Henge XI, 2019
Acrylic and oil on canvas
240 × 285 cm
(94.5 × 112.2 ins)

p.23
Henge IV, 2018–2019
Acrylic and oil on canvas
240 × 285 cm
(94.5 × 112.2 ins)

p.25
Henge V, 2017
Acrylic and oil on canvas
240 × 285 cm
(94.5 × 112.2 ins)

p.27
Henge XII, 2019
Acrylic and oil on canvas
240 × 285 cm
(94.5 × 112.2 ins)

p.29
Henge XVI, 2020–2021
Acrylic and oil on canvas
240 × 285 cm
(94.5 × 112.2 ins)

p.31
Henge VI, 2019–2021
Acrylic and oil on canvas
240 × 285 cm
(94.5 × 112.2 ins)

p.33
Henge VII, 2019–2022
Acrylic and oil on canvas
240 × 285 cm
(94.5 × 112.2 ins)

p.35
Henge XIV, 2020–2021
Acrylic and oil on canvas
240 × 285 cm
(94.5 × 112.2 ins)

p.39
Henge XXVIII, 2021–2022
Acrylic and oil on canvas
180 × 215 cm
(71 × 84.6 ins)

p.40
Henge XXXII, 2021–2022
Acrylic and oil on canvas
180 × 215 cm
(71 × 84.6 ins)

p.41
Henge XXXV, 2022
Acrylic and oil on canvas
180 × 215 cm
(71 × 84.6 ins)

p.42
Henge XIX, 2020–2021
Acrylic and oil on canvas
125 × 135 cm
(49.2 × 53.1 ins)

p.43
Henge XVIII, 2020–2021
Acrylic and oil on canvas
125 × 135 cm
(49.2 × 53.1 ins)

p.44
Henge XXXIII, 2021–2022
Acrylic and oil on canvas
125 × 135 cm
(49.2 × 53.1 ins)

p.45
Henge XVII, 2021–2022
Acrylic and oil on canvas
180 × 215 cm
(71 × 84.6 ins)

p.47
Henge X, 2017
Acrylic and oil on canvas
180 × 215 cm
(71 × 84.6 ins)

p.48
Henge XX, 2020–2021
Acrylic and oil on canvas
180 × 215 cm
(71 × 84.6 ins)

p.49
Henge XXXIV, 2021–2022
Acrylic and oil on canvas
125 × 135 cm
(49.2 × 53.1 ins)

pp.50–51
Henge VIII, 2019
Acrylic and oil on canvas
180 × 215 cm
(71 × 84.6 ins)

Works on Paper

p.55
Henge No. 8, 2021
Watercolour, gouache and pencil
on handmade paper
38 × 43 cm
(15 × 17 ins)

p.56
Henge No. 4, 2021
Watercolour, gouache and pencil
on handmade paper
38 × 43 cm
(15 × 17 ins)

p.57
Henge No. 2, 2021
Watercolour, gouache and pencil
on handmade paper
38 × 43 cm
(15 × 17 ins)

p.58
Henge No. 3, 2021
Watercolour, gouache and pencil
on handmade paper
38 × 43 cm
(15 × 17 ins)

p.59
Henge No. 7, 2021
Watercolour, gouache and pencil
on handmade paper
38 × 43 cm
(15 × 17 ins)

p.60
Henge No. 6, 2021
Watercolour, gouache and pencil
on handmade paper
38 × 43 cm
(15 × 17 ins)

p.61
Henge No. 5, 2021
Watercolour, gouache and pencil
on handmade paper
38 × 43 cm
(15 × 17 ins)

p.62
Henge No. 1, 2021
Watercolour, gouache and pencil
on handmade paper
38 × 43 cm
(15 × 17 ins)

p.63
Henge No. 9, 2021
Watercolour, gouache and pencil
on handmade paper
38 × 43 cm
(15 × 17 ins)

pp.4, 75–83
10 Stones
From a series of black and white analogue
photographs taken by the artist at the Neolithic
Henge Monument, Avebury, 2017.

Chronology

1946 Born 30 November in the small seaside resort Withernsea on the east coast of Yorkshire.

1965 Moves to London to study English Literature at the Avery Hill College, taking art as a subsidiary subject.

1967 Writes his dissertation on 'Suspended Forms' in the work of Anthony Caro and Victor Pasmore.

1970 Takes his first studio at SPACE, St Katharine Docks, an artists' collective set up by Peter Sedgley and Bridget Riley.

1973 First solo exhibition in London at the Institute of Contemporary Arts.

1974 Moves his studio to Martello Street in East London where he continues to work until the early 90s.

1977 First exhibition at Nigel Greenwood Gallery, London where he will exhibit for the next 10 years.

1979 Travels to the Shetland and Faroe Islands, commencing a practice he still maintains of keeping journals/ sketch books and taking photographs while travelling.

1980 Awarded an Arts Council of Great Britain scholarship to work for a year as a guest of the Walker Art Gallery, Liverpool.

1981 Awarded a scholarship, funded partly by Kunsthalle Nuremberg, to work in Germany followed by an exhibition at Kunsthalle Nuremberg in 1982.

1982 Returns to London. Publishes *Black and White... or How to Paint with a Hammer* in collaboration with Matt's Gallery, London.

1984 Awarded a Calouste Gulbenkian Print Bursary to produce his first lithographic prints.

1985 Visits the painter Joan Mitchell at her studio at Vétheuil, near Paris. Commences the *Lapland Paintings* (1985–86).

1988 Completes *A History of Rocks* (1986–88), the last body of work in which the artist will integrate a photographic element. All 40 works are installed in 1989 at Kunstforum, Städtische Galerie im Lenbachhaus, Munich. Travels to Greenland with the art critic Timo Valjakka.

1989 Awarded the German DAAD scholarship to live and work in West Berlin for one year, staying on subsequently to finish the *Diptychs* paintings (1983–1990).

1990 A major mid-career retrospective exhibition, curated by Catherine Lampert, takes place at the Whitechapel Art Gallery, London.

1991 Travels to Papua New Guinea with the Dutch sculptor Waldo Bien. Purchases a farm in Hartgrove, Dorset where he continues to live and work.

1992 Appointed Lecturer in Postgraduate Painting at the Slade School of Fine Art, University College, London. Begins his *Hartgrove Paintings* (1992–94). Travels to Vienna to visit his Austrian painter friend Kurt Kocherscheidt.

1993 Guest Professor at the Staatliche Hochschule für Bildende Künste, Frankfurt.

1995 Travels to eastern Siberia with the Finnish ecologist Yrjö Haila and curator Marketta Seppälä. The three monumental *Marianne North Paintings* (1994–95) are exhibited at Matt's Gallery, London.

1996 Returns to eastern Siberia. A retrospective exhibition of his *Works on Paper 1980–1996* is organised by University of Brighton Gallery. Visits Lebanon as guest of his gallerist Naila Kunigk.

2000 Spends two months at the Josef and Anni Albers Foundation, Bethany, Connecticut.

2001 Begins the *Four Quartets Paintings* (2001–07). Retrospective painting exhibition, curated by Karsten Ohrt, at the Kunsthallen Brandts, Odense, Denmark.

2003 Elected a member of the Royal Academy of Arts, London.

2004 Spends four weeks travelling in China at the invitation of the Red Mansion Foundation, London. Begins work on his *Temple Paintings* (2004–06), which will constitute one part of his *Four Quartets Paintings*.

2005 Returns to China to continue travelling and participates in the exhibition *Seven Royal Academicians in China* at the National Art Gallery, Beijing, the Shanghai Museum and the Royal Academy of Arts, London. Retrospective painting exhibition at the Morat Institute, Freiburg, Germany. *In Praise of Painting: Three Essays* is published by University of Brighton.

2006 Returns to Russia, travelling to Novgorod and St. Petersburg to look specifically at the icons of Andrei Rublev. Appointed Professor of Drawing (2006–11) at the Royal Academy Schools of Arts, London.

2007 The definite group of *Four Quartets Paintings* (2001–07) is exhibited at the Morat Institute in Freiburg, Germany. Travels with his son to eastern Turkey and Cappadocia to visit early Christian sites.

2008 Returns to Turkey and continues to Syria. Travels to Cambodia at the invitation of his gallerist Susanne Ottesen.

2009 Resumes working with photographs, some of which are exhibited alongside his *Hartgrove Paintings* at the Artists' Laboratory 01, Royal Academy of Arts, London in 2010. Commences work on the *Twelve Standing* paintings (2009–12).

2011 A retrospective of the artist's black paintings *Black and Black again… Paintings 1987–2010*, curated by Ove Mogensen, takes place at Kunstmuseet i Tønder, Denmark.

2012 Retrospective exhibition, curated by Heinz Liesbrock, at the Josef Albers Museum, Quadrat, Bottrop, Germany.

2014 Commences work on the *Portrait of a Woman* paintings (2014–16). Installs the site-specific work *Hours of Darkness, Hours of Light* (2012–14) at Kunst-Station Sankt Peter, Cologne. Retrospective exhibition *Against Photography: Early Works 1975–1990* at HackelBury Fine Art, London. Exhibits *Twelve Standing* paintings at Horsens Kunstmuseum, Denmark.

2015 Continues his travels to Andalucía, Spain and Morocco.

2016 Begins working on the *Henge* paintings.

2017 The site-specific installation *Against Architecture* is shown at Matt's Gallery, London.

2018 Exhibits works from the *Henge* paintings series together with sculptures by Richard Deacon at Galleri Susanne Ottesen, Copenhagen. Retrospective exhibition *Paintings 1992–2017* at the Ferens Art Gallery in Hull, his childhood city museum.

2020 Exhibits four of the large *Henge* paintings together with sculptures by Tony Cragg at Skulpturenpark Waldfrieden, Wuppertal, Germany.

Selected One-person Exhibitions

2022

Henge Paintings, Galleri Susanne Ottesen, Copenhagen

Henge Paintings, Heather Gaudio Fine Art, New Canaan, Connecticut

2021

Hours, Paintings 2019–2021, GSA Gallery, Stockholm

2020

Ian McKeever Malerei. Tony Cragg Skulpturen, Skulpturenpark Waldfrieden, Wuppertal, Germany

2019

The Nature of Painting, Heather Gaudio Fine Art, New Canaan, Connecticut

2018

Ian McKeever & Richard Deacon, Galleri Susanne Ottesen, Copenhagen

Weight and Measure, Prints 1993–2018, Young Gallery, Salisbury

Paintings 1992–2018, Ferens Art Gallery, Hull

2017

Against Architecture Installation, Matt's Gallery, London

Paintings and Painted Panels, Gallery Andersson Sandström, Stockholm

2016

Portrait of a Woman, Paintings 2014–2016, Galleri Susanne Ottesen, Copenhagen

...and the sky dreamt it was the sea, HackelBury Fine Art, London

Twelve Standing, Galerie Forsblom, Helsinki

2015

Hours of Darkness, Hours of Light, Kunstmuseet i Tønder, Denmark

Between Darkness and Light, National Gallery of the Faroe Islands, Tørshavn

2014

Hours of Darkness, Hours of Light, Kunst-Station Sankt Peter, Cologne, Germany

Twelve Standing and *Three*, Horsens Kunstmuseum, Denmark
Eagduru – Against Architecture, Galleri Susanne Ottesen, Copenhagen
Against Photography: Early Works 1975–1990, HackelBury Fine Art, London

2013
Twelve Standing, Galleri Andersson Sandström, Stockholm

2012
Hartgrove: Paintings and Photographs, Josef Albers Museum, Quadrat, Bottrop, Germany

2011
Black and Black again… Paintings 1987–2010, Kunstmuseet i Tønder, Denmark

2010
Hartgrove, Paintings and Photographs, Artists' Laboratory 01, Royal Academy of Arts, London
Hartgrove, Paintings and Photographs, Galleri Susanne Ottesen, Copenhagen

2009
Assembly, Paintings 2006–2008, Galerie Forsblom, Helsinki
Recent Paintings, Galleri Andersson Sandström, Stockholm
Temple Paintings, Kings Place Gallery, London

2007
Four Quartets, Paintings 2001–2007, Morat-Institut, Freiburg i.Br., Germany
Assembly, Paintings 2002–2007, Kunsthallen Brandts, Odense, Denmark

2006
New Paintings, Galerie Forsblom, Helsinki
Whispers, 48 Drawings 2004–2005, Ny Carlsberg Glyptotek, Copenhagen
Temple Paintings, Galerie Susanne Ottesen, Copenhagen

2005
Bilder 1983–93, Morat-Institut, Freiburg i.Br., Germany

2004
Sentinel, Recent Paintings and Works on Paper, Alan Cristea Gallery, London
Recent Paintings and Ten Years of Drawing, Kettle's Yard, University of Cambridge

2003
Watercolours and Gouaches 1993–2003, Nordiska Akvarellmuseet, Skärhamn, Sweden

2002
Paintings from the Four Quartets Series, Horsens Kunstmuseum, Denmark
William Blake's 'Jerusalem', The Emanation of the Giant Albion, Alan Cristea Gallery, London
Self-Shadow, Paintings, Galerie Stadtpark, Krems, Austria

2001
Paintings 1993–2000, Kunsthallen Brandts, Odense, Denmark

2000
Paintings and Works on Paper, Alan Cristea Gallery, London

1997
Paintings 1990–1996, Porin Taidemuseo, Pori, Finland
Recent Paintings, Galería Módulo, Lisbon
Recent Paintings, Galerie Tanit, Munich
Colour Etchings, Monoprints and One Painting, Alan Cristea Gallery, London

1996
Hour Paintings, Galerie Elisabeth Kaufmann, Basle, Switzerland
Works on Paper 1981–1996, University of Brighton and The Terrace Gallery, Harewood House, Leeds

1995
The Marianne North Paintings, Matt's Gallery, London
Recent Paintings and Drawings, The Haggerty Museum of Art, Milwaukee, Wisconsin

1994
Hartgrove Paintings, Bernard Jacobson Gallery, London
Hour Paintings, Galerie Tanit, Munich, Germany

1993
Hour Paintings, Stephen Solovy Gallery, Chicago, Illinois
1992
Door Paintings, Galerie Stadtpark, Krems, Austria
Door Paintings, Galería Módulo, Lisbon
Recent Paintings, Galerie Elisabeth Kaufmann, Basle, Switzerland
1990
Notes 1989–1990, DAAD Galerie, West Berlin
Large Diptychs, Galerie Tanit, Cologne, Germany
Paintings 1978–1990, Whitechapel Art Gallery, London
1989
A History of Rocks 1986–1988, Kunstforum, Städtische Galerie im Lenbachhaus, Munich
1987
The Staffa Project, A Collaboration, Ian McKeever and Thomas Joshua Cooper, Harris Museum and Art Gallery, Preston; Provincial Museum Hasselt, Belgium; Arnolfini, Bristol; Glasgow Art Gallery and Museum Kelvingrove, Glasgow
Recent Paintings, Galleria Krista Mikkola, Helsinki
Ian McKeever im Innsbrucker Kunstverein, Kunstverein Innsbruck, Austria
Echo and Reflection, Arbeiten 1983–1987, Kunstverein Braunschweig, Germany
1986
Lapland Paintings, Nigel Greenwood Gallery, London
Through the Ice Lens, Galerie Tanit, Munich
1985
Traditional Landscapes and Works on Paper, Galerie Nächst St. Stephan, Vienna
Borderlines – Abstracting Art from Nature, Arnolfini Bristol (with Frank Auerbach)
1984
Traditional Landscapes, Galerie Tanit, Munich
Recent Paintings, John Hansard Gallery, University of Southampton
1983
Traditional Landscapes, Nigel Greenwood Gallery, London
1982
Deutscher Zyklus, Kunsthalle Nuremberg, Germany
Neue Arbeiten, Galerie Arno Kohnen, Düsseldorf, Germany
Black and White... or How to Paint with a Hammer, Matt's Gallery, London
1981
Paintings: Islands and Night Flak Series, Walker Art Gallery, Liverpool and Museum of Modern Art, Oxford
1980
Fields, Waterfalls and Birds, Arnolfini Bristol; Third Eye Centre Glasgow and ICA, London
Aspects of Work 1973–1980, Walker Art Gallery, Liverpool
Ian McKeever, Galleria del Cavallino, Venice, Italy
1979
Field Series 1978, Nigel Greenwood Gallery, London
1978
Sand and Sea Series, Richard Demarco Gallery, Edinburgh; Spectro Arts, Newcastle and Galleria Foksal, Warsaw
1977
Sand and Sea Series, Nigel Greenwood Gallery, London and Galleria Tommaseo, Trieste, Italy
1976
Works 1974–76, Galleria del Cavallino, Venice, Italy
1973
Ian McKeever, Institute of Contemporary Arts, London
1971
Ian McKeever, Cardiff Arts Centre

Selected Group Exhibitions

2022
Spectacular Unimposing, Künstlerhaus Bregenz, Austria
2019
Towards the Sublime, Galerie Tanit, Beirut, Lebanon
Searching For Identity, Trieste Contemporanea, Studio Tommaseo, Trieste, Italy
2017
Air: Visualising the Invisible in British Art, 1868–2017, The Royal West of England Academy, Bristol
On Photography, Galleri Susanne Ottesen, Copenhagen
Abstract Minds, Braun-Falco Gallery, Munich
2015
Qwaypurlake, Hauser & Wirth Somerset, UK
2014
Structures, British and German Painting in Dialogue, Kunsthalle Wilhelmshaven, Germany
Some Artists' Artists, Marian Goodman Gallery, New York
2013
Gifted, From the Royal Academy to the Queen, Royal Collection Trust, London
2012
Prism: Drawings from 1990–2011, National Museum of Norway, Oslo
2011
Watercolour, Tate Britain, London
Royal Academicians, Seongnam Arts Center, South Korea
2005
Seven Royal Academicians in China, National Art Gallery, Beijing; Shanghai Art Museum and Royal Academy of Arts, London
Matisse to Freud, A Critic's Choice: The Alexander Walker Bequest, The British Museum London and Hayward Gallery Touring
The Art of White, The Lowry, Manchester
2004
Works and Days, Acquisitions for the Louisiana Collection 2000–2004, Louisiana Museum of Modern Art, Humlebæk, Denmark
2003
In Print, Hakodate Museum of Art and Marugame Museum of Contemporary Art, Shikoku Island, Japan
2002
Centenary Exhibition, Carlsberg Foundation, Glyptotek, Copenhagen
In Print, The Art Pavilion Gallery, Belgrade, Serbia and Yaroslavl Museum of Fine Art, Yaroslavl, Russia
1999
Graphic! British Prints Now, Yale Centre for British Art, New Haven, Connecticut, USA
Into the Light, Photographic Printing Out of the Darkroom, The Royal Photographic Society, Bath; Calcografia Nacional, Madrid and Fundacion Municipal de Cultura, Valladolid, Spain
1996
Strangers in the Arctic, Rundetårn, Copenhagen; Museum of Contemporary Art, Helsinki and The Art Gallery of Ontario, Toronto, Canada
Nuevas Abstracciones, Museo Nacional Centro de Arte, Reina Sofia, Madrid; Museu d'Art Contemporani de Barcelona, Spain and Kunsthalle Bielefeld, Germany
1995
Contemporary British Art in Print, Scottish National Gallery of Modern Art, Edinburgh; Yale Centre for British Art, New Haven, Connecticut and McNay Art Museum, San Antonio, Texas
Life Patterns, Tate Gallery, London
From Picasso to Woodrow, New Acquisitions of Prints, Tate Gallery, London
1992
Geteilte Bilder: das Diptychon in der neuen Kunst, Museum Folkwang, Essen, Germany

Des Dessin, Museum für Gegenwartskunst, Basle, Switzerland
Tierra de Nadie, Hospital Real, Granada, Spain
Aus der Sammlung. Seit 25 Jahren, Kunsthalle Nuremberg, Germany

1991
Nature, Création du Peintre, Musée Cantonal des Beaux-Arts, Lausanne, Switzerland

1990
Le Paysage, Trace de la Mémoire, Galerie Barbar & Cie, Paris, France

1989
Landschaft in der Erfahrung, Kölnischer Kunstverein, Cologne, Germany
Synnyt: Sources of Contemporary Art, Museum of Contemporary Art, Helsinki

1988
ROSC '88, Guinness Hop Store, Dublin
New British Painting, Contemporary Arts Center, Cincinnati, Ohio
Zurück zur Natur, aber wie? Städtische Galerie im Prinz-Max-Palais, Karlsruhe, Germany
A British View, Koplin Gallery, Los Angeles, California

1987
Current Affairs – British Painting and Sculpture in the 80s, Museum of Modern Art, Oxford; Műcsarnok, Budapest, Hungary; Národní Galerie, Prague, Czech Republic and Zacheta, National Gallery of Art, Warsaw
British Art of the 1980s, Liljevalchs Konsthall, Stockholm and Sara Hildénin Taidemuseo, Tampere, Finland
Viewpoint: British Art of the 1980s, Musées Royaux d'Art et d'Histoire, Brussels, Belgium

1986
British Painting 1986, Künstlerhaus Vienna
Prospect '86, Frankfurter Kunstverein/ Schirn Kunsthalle Frankfurt

1985
4. Europäische Grafik-Biennale, Baden-Baden, Germany
A Journey through Contemporary Art with Nigel Greenwood, Hayward Annual 1985, Hayward Gallery, London
Ambiguities and Characters, Konsthall Landskrona, Sweden
Dialogue, Moderna Museet, Stockholm
Living Art, Guinness Hop Store, Dublin
Steirischer Herbst '85 – Phase II: Das Bild einer Ausstellung, Stadtmuseum Graz, Austria

1984
British Art Show 2...Old Allegiances and New Directions 1979–84, Ikon Gallery, Birmingham and Royal Scottish Academy, Edinburgh

1983
The Granada Collection – New British Painting and Drawing, Whitworth Art Gallery, University of Manchester
Z.B. Landschaft, Bonner Kunstverein, Bonn, Germany
Art Itinera 1983, Castello Pasquini, Castiglioncello, Volterra, Italy

1981
Art and the Sea, Institute of Contemporary Arts, London

1980
Paesaggio di Paesaggi, Salone degli Specchi del Teatro Comunale, Milan

1979
Zeichen-Triennale, Kunsthalle Nuremberg, Germany
Photographic Works, Galleria Cannaviello, Milan

1976
Englische Landschaftsmalerei, Badischer Kunstverein, Karlsruhe; Haus am Waldsee, Berlin and Kunsthalle Wilhelmshaven, Germany

1975
From Britain '75, Taidehalli Helsinki, Alvar Aalto-Museo, Jyväskylä and Taidemuseo, Tampere, Finland

Selected Publications

Ian McKeever, *A History of Rocks 1986–1988*, texts by Helmut Friedel and Lynne Cooke, Kunstforum, Städtische Galerie im Lenbachhaus, Munich, 1989

Ian McKeever, *Paintings 1978–1990*, texts by Lewis Biggs, Wulf Herzogenrath and Wolfgang Max Faust, Whitechapel Art Gallery, London, 1990

Ian McKeever, *Paintings*, (monograph), texts by Marjorie Allthorpe-Guyton, Michael Tucker and Catherine Lampert, Lund Humphries, London, 2005

Ian McKeever, *In Praise of Painting*, three essays, University of Brighton, 2005

Ian McKeever, *Four Quartets, Malerei Paintings 2001–2007*, text by Martin Caiger-Smith, Morat-Institut für Kunst und Kunstwissenschaft, Freiburg and Verlag der Buchhandlung Walther König, Cologne, 2007

Artists' Laboratory Ian McKeever RA 01, *Hartgrove Paintings and Photographs*, text by Norbert Lynton and Ian McKeever in conversation with Richard Deacon, Royal Academy of Arts, London, 2010

Ian McKeever, *Hartgrove, Malerei und Fotografie*, text by Heinz Liesbrock, Josef Albers Museum. Quadrat Bottrop and Verlag der Buchhandlung Walther König, Cologne, 2012

Ian McKeever, *Against Photography: Early Works 1975–1990*, text by Mark Prince, imprint #1, HackelBury Fine Art, London, 2014

Galleri Susanne Ottesen
Gothersgade 49
1123 Copenhagen
Denmark
www.susanneottesen.dk

Heather Gaudio Fine Art
66 Elm Street
New Canaan
CT 06840
United States
www.heathergaudiofineart.com

Co-ordinated by Gerlinde Gabriel
Proofreading: Allegra Nancini Barker, Gerlinde Gabriel and Aimee Selby
Design: Tim Harvey, London
Print: Narayana Press

Photo credits
Jonathan Bassett: pp.17–35, 39–49, 55–63
Installation photos:
Michael Richter, reproduced by permission of the Cragg Foundation, pp.36–37, 68–69
Stine Heger, courtesy Galleri Susanne Ottesen, pp.50–51, 71
Ian McKeever, pp.4, 75–83

First published in 2022 by Anomie Publishing, London
www.anomie-publishing.com

A catalogue record for this book is available from the British Library

ISBN 978-1-910221-41-9

Printed in Denmark

Distributed by Casemate Art

jacket
Henge I, 2017–2019 (detail)